Academic Study Skills: An Introduction

Nicoleta Mariana Iftimie

Ann Wan-lih Chang

封面設計：實踐大學教務處出版組

出 版 心 語

　　近年來，全球數位出版蓄勢待發，美國從事數位出版的業者超過百家，亞洲數位出版的新勢力也正在起飛，諸如日本、中國大陸都方興未艾，而台灣卻被視為數位出版的處女地，有極大的開發拓展空間。植基於此，本組自民國 93 年 9 月起，即醞釀規劃以數位出版模式，協助本校專任教師致力於學術出版，以激勵本校研究風氣，提昇教學品質及學術水準。

　　在規劃初期，調查得知秀威資訊科技股份有限公司是採行數位印刷模式並做數位少量隨需出版〔POD＝Print on Demand〕（含編印銷售發行）的科技公司，亦為中華民國政府出版品正式授權的 POD 數位處理中心，尤其該公司可提供「免費學術出版」形式，相當符合本組推展數位出版的立意。隨即與秀威公司密集接洽，雙方就數位出版服務要點、數位出版申請作業流程、出版發行合約書以及出版合作備忘錄等相關事宜逐一審慎研擬，歷時 9 個月，至民國 94 年 6 月始告順利簽核公布。

執行迄今逾 2 年，承蒙本校謝董事長孟雄、謝校長宗興、劉教務長麗雲、藍教授秀璋以及秀威公司宋總經理政坤等多位長官給予本組全力的支持與指導，本校諸多教師亦身體力行，主動提供學術專著委由本組協助數位出版，數量達 20 本，在此一併致上最誠摯的謝意。諸般溫馨滿溢，將是挹注本組持續推展數位出版的最大動力。

本出版團隊由葉立誠組長、王雯珊老師、賴怡勳老師三人為組合，以極其有限的人力，充分發揮高效能的團隊精神，合作無間，各司統籌策劃、協商研擬、視覺設計等職掌，在精益求精的前提下，至望弘揚本校實踐大學的校譽，具體落實出版機能。

實踐大學教務處出版組　謹識

97 年 9 月

2008.09

CONTENTS

UNIVERSITY LIFE...7

PREPARING TO STUDY..19

STUDY AIDS...33

NOTE-TAKING...53

SUMMARIZING..69

TYPES OF ORAL PRESENTATIONS..83

MAKING ORAL PRESENTATIONS..95

WRITING RESEARCH PAPERS...115

BASIC RESEARCH SKILLS..131

CREATING A BIBLIOGRAPHY...149

PREPARING FOR EXAMS...159

UNIVERSITY LIFE

Schools and Universities

? **1** *You are now a university student. You have already noticed several differences between high school life and culture and university culture. How are they different? Work in groups of three or four to complete this table:*

Differences	High School	University
Students' age		
Students generally live…		
No of classes/week		
Subjects (general or specialized?)		
Optional courses		
Students' autonomy		
Teachers (native or foreign)		
Teaching styles		
Assignments		
Exams		
Others (please specify)		

As you can see, there are differences between high school culture and university culture. One of the most important is that now you prepare for your major and your future career, so the courses you take belong to special fields of study. At university level you have more time for independent study, which means that you are expected to use the materials you can find in the library or other sources to prepare your assignments and exams. There is now a shift to independent study, learning autonomy and responsibility for your own learning. The assignments and reports that university students have to prepare are longer and much better informed than those prepared by high school students and they will represent a certain percentage in your final grade. Such reports should meet certain requirements concerning content, but also length, layout, structure, style.

The University

As a freshman you need to familiarize yourself with the university and its surroundings. In many Western countries, there is a so-called *Orientation Day* during which freshmen are being shown the various buildings, offices and facilities on campus and are presented general information on living and studying at that university.

2 *In the space provided below, draw a map of your university campus. Use rectangles* ☐ *for the buildings and orient them according to the cardinal points (north, south, east or west). Label the buildings using names or letters.*
If necessary, go out and find the exact position of each building.

My University Campus

```
                           North




West                                                    East




                           South
```

Check with a partner. Are your maps similar or different? Surf the internet to find the map of your campus. Compare this map to the one you have drawn.

3 *Work with a partner. Use your map to ask and answer questions about the offices and departments that can be found in each building on your university campus.*

Student A:
1. What can you find in the northern part of the campus?
2. Which buildings are situated in the east? What offices/ departments/ classrooms are in these buildings?
3. Are there any student dorms? Where are they situated?
4. Your own question.
5. Your own question.

Student B:
1. What can you find in the southern part of the campus?
2. Which buildings are situated in the west? What offices/ departments/ classrooms are in these buildings?
3. Where is the library? How many floors does it have?
4. Your own question.
5. Your own question.

University Divisions
The big divisions of a university are:
1. the campus
2. the colleges (faculties)
3. the departments

4 *Match each university division with its definition:*

1. ___campus	a. that part of the university that teaches your subject
2. ___college	b. the place where your university is
3. ___department	c. offices that provide advice, information and help to students and staff
4. ___administrative offices	d. a group of departments teaching related subjects

The Campus

The campus represents the place where all your university buildings are. One and the same university can have more than one campus. The university campuses can be situated in the same city, in different cities of the same country and even in different countries. Therefore, when you apply to study at your university you may find out that you have your *Introduction to Literature* course in one campus and the *British and American Culture* course in another campus.

 **5** *1. Think about your university. How many campuses does it have? If it has more than one, where are they situated? Complete the appropriate box(es).*

My University				
1 campus	More campuses			
	Number	Situated		
		Same city	Different cities (same country)	Different countries

2. If your university has got more campuses, where do you have classes now? Do you have to go to different campuses?

The College

The university is usually divided into a number of colleges / faculties. A college/faculty is a group of departments teaching related subjects. American English uses the term *college* for such divisions, e.g. College of Arts, College of Management, while British English uses the term *faculty*, e.g. Faculty of Medicine, Faculty of Letters. In American English, on the other hand, the word *faculty* refers to the teaching staff at a university.

Many colleges/faculties have their own smaller library, which makes it easier for students to find books and other materials related to the subjects they study, especially when the university library is far away.

6 *How many colleges are in your university? Do you know how they are called?*

The Department

The smallest division in a university is the department. Each department teaches a certain subject, e.g. English, History, Finance, etc. Within each department there can be several smaller sections to it. For example, in the Department of English there could be a section of Literature, another of Linguistics, another of ELT (English Language Teaching) or of Translation.

When you study for a major, most courses are probably taught in one department; some minor courses, however, can be taught in other departments.

Your teachers belong to a particular department where they have their department/staff room, meetings and offices.

 7 *Answer these questions:*

1. How many departments are there in your college/faculty?
2. How are they called?
3. Which department do most of your teachers belong to?
4. Where is this department situated (building, floor, room number)?

Administrative Offices

All universities have certain offices that offer various services, help and advice to students and teachers.

 8 *Work with a partner. Name 3 administrative offices on your campus.*

1. _____

2. _____

3. _____

?9 *Below you can find some administrative offices that are usually found in a university.*

1. Match each office with the kind of service it provides.

Office	Service
1. ___Student affairs office	a. • helps overseas (foreign) students to fill in application forms • gives them information about admission requirements, fees and scholarships.
2. ___Academic affairs office	b. • answers questions about compulsory and optional courses in that department • tells you where to find teaching staff
3. ___Human resources office	c. provides servicing for on-campus computers
4. ___International office	d. calculates salaries for personnel
5. ___Computer center	e. provides daycare for the pre-school children of staff
6. ___Department office	f. • registers students • provides information on courses taught in the university • provides the list of students enrolled for each course • makes sure the students' final grades are recorded in due time
7. ___Accommodation service	g. gives help with various general problems that may appear on campus (e.g. if the air conditioning system in your room is broken)
8. ___Childcare service	h. organizes accommodation in the university dorms
9. ___General affairs office	i. • offers general support and advice to students • gives information about extracurricular activities • may list part-time jobs available for students on campus
10. ___ Accounting office	j. helps the personnel in the university with various problems (contract, accommodation, etc)

Facilities

Universities also have various facilities that either help students with their studies or give them the possibility to spend their free time.

Usually such facilities include:

• a library and reading rooms

- lecture hall/ auditorium/ conference facilities
- bookstore
- gym
- outdoor sports courts
- swimming pool
- restaurants
- cafeteria
- convenience stores

? **10** *1. Which of the above-mentioned facilities can be found in your campus? Place a tick (√) if your answer is "yes".*
2. Where are these facilities placed? Look at the map you have drawn and ask your partner questions about the location of such facilities.

People
In all universities, campuses, colleges and departments you meet staff: teachers and administrators.

The University Leaders
There are some people in the university whom you will probably not meet in person. You will probably see them on School Day, at the graduation ceremony and other formal occasions.
The university leader may be called in different ways depending on the country.
Thus, in America, the university leader is called *president*. In Great Britain, he/she is called a *vice-chancellor*, while in some other European countries he is called *rector.*

? **11** *Is your university leader called a president, vice-chancellor or rector?*

The head of a college or faculty is called a dean. Deans are elected or nominated usually for a fixed period of time (two or four years), after which they generally return to their department and continue teaching.

The head of a department is called chair or head of department. They are either elected by the department staff or appointed by the leaders of the university. Chairs have an administrative role, but they also teach.

The Department Staff
The titles of people teaching in a department may differ from one country and even from one university to another.

Taiwan:
Professor
Associate Professor
Assistant Professor
Lecturer

North America:
Professor
Associate Professor
Assistant Professor
Instructor (sometimes "Lecturer")
Teaching Assistant

Great Britain:
Professor
Reader
Senior Lecturer
Lecturer

Romania:
Research and teaching staff (higher rank)
Professor ("profesor")
Associate professor ("conferentiar")
Assistant professor ("lector" or "sef de lucrari")

Teaching staff (lower rank):
Teaching assistant ("asistent")
Junior teaching assistant ("preparator")

Administrative Staff
When enrolling and after that, as an undergraduate student, you will meet not only teachers, but also non-teaching, administrative staff. They have various titles, such as registrar, secretary, administrative assistant, office manager, international relations officer, university/student counselor. Their job is to help you enroll, apply for courses, find your way around and generally help you solve various problems that you may encounter. They work in various offices of the university.

Contacting Staff

Sometimes you need to contact university staff (teachers and administrative staff) for various reasons connected to your studies.

?12 *1. In the table below, check (√) the university staff you have already contacted (teaching and/or administrative staff) and specify the reasons you have contacted them for. Check the teaching staff box only in case you contacted your teachers **outside class**.*

Reasons	Teaching Staff	Administrative Staff

2. Below there are some reasons why students may contact university staff. Read them and add (some of) them to your table, if necessary.

The main reasons for contacting university staff are:
- enrolling in a university
- asking information about courses you need/want to take
- leaving a course
- applying for a grant
- paying your student fees
- asking your teachers questions about the lectures
- asking about assignments
- applying for a part-time job on campus
- enrolling in extra-curricular activities
- asking for personal references/recommendations

How to Contact Staff

There are various ways in which you can contact the university staff:

1. Going to the office
   This is a manner of meeting both administrative and teaching staff.

All the administrative offices in a university have a daily program. This program is usually printed on the office door. Make sure you know what this program is before entering.

Your teachers can be contacted during their 'Office hours.' The teachers will tell you about their office hours at the beginning of each semester. In case you have forgotten, you can ask the secretary of your department or you can go to the university website.

2. Telephoning

Telephoning is still used by students to contact their teachers. Sometimes teachers ask you to fix an appointment via telephone. In such a case, you should first phone the teacher to fix an appointment, then visit him/her in the office. Remember that telephone calls may be rather disturbing if the staff member is doing work or if he/she is just talking to someone who has made an appointment. Therefore, before you ring, make sure there is no other way of contacting that person. Also remember to keep your telephone call short and to the point.

3. Emailing

Emailing is nowadays a convenient way of communicating with staff and classmates.

You can use the e-mail to ask your teachers questions about the course, assignments, to fix a meeting, etc. If you want to send assignments or reports via e-mail, check if you are allowed to do so.

When writing an e-mail to your teachers, you should respect some rules of etiquette, such as

- Write a clear 'Subject' to your e-mail, such as "Appointment" or "Can I get an extension?" or "Thesis".
- Start your e-mail with a salutation, such as "Dear Prof. Jones", "Dear Dr. Jones", "Dear Teacher" or simply "Dear Peter", depending on the way you generally address that teacher.
- Make it clear who you are and what you are writing for. The other person cannot see you and may not know who you are by simply looking at your e-mail address.
- Make sure you are polite. The other person cannot see you, so it is easy to offend someone.
- It is polite to end by thanking the receiver for taking the time to read and answer your e-mail.
- If you send documents, such as (parts of) assignments, reports or a thesis, make sure you place them in the attachment.
- It is better not to send large file attachments because
  - it is usually tiring for someone (including teachers) to read many pages directly from the computer screen
  - it is **not** your teachers' responsibility to print out your paper

- when your assignment/article/paper needs more detailed feedback, it is sometimes difficult and time consuming for the teacher to give his/her feedback via e-mail. A meeting could be more beneficial in this case.

University Life: Matches and Mismatches
You have already realized that there are differences between high school and university life. You should also be aware of the fact that there are differences between university cultures from one country to another and sometimes even from one university to another.

? 13 *In the chart below you can find some information on 'Western' universities. Think of your* university. Are things similar or different?

'Western' Universities	Your University	
	Similar	**Different**
Students arrive at the last minute, but **before** the teacher.		
Students seat where they want.		
Nobody stands for the professor.		
The professor may greet the students, but the students don't usually answer.		
There are several types of courses: • *Lectures*, during which the professor talks and a large group of students (150-200) take notes. • *Seminars/Discussion* classes, during which smaller groups of students (10-25) discuss assigned topics with a tutor or teaching assistant. • *Lab classes* during which science majors or medical students perform experiments.		
During seminars/ discussion groups, students express their own ideas, which may sometimes be different from those of the teacher.		
For their exams, students need both to attend lectures and read their textbooks.		
Assessment methods include		

• Continuous assessment (coursework, tests, projects, seminar participation) • Midterm exam (in some countries) • Final Exam		
Duration of undergraduate programs • Normally 3 years (European Union) • Normally 4 years (USA)		

PREPARING TO STUDY

Are you a successful student? Are the results you obtain in accordance with the time and effort you allot for studying? In order to become aware of your own attitude to learning, try to answer this quiz.

1 Quiz

For each of the following statements, check "Yes" if it applies to you or "No" if it doesn't.

1. I enjoy studying.
   Yes__   No__

2. When I study for an exam, I first try to understand all the ideas, express them in my own words and I never memorize word for word.
   Yes__   No__

3. I usually postpone studying until the night before the exam.
   Yes__   No__

4. Even if I study enough for an exam, when I see the questions my mind goes blank.
   Yes__   No__

5. In class my mind wanders around, I cannot concentrate and I sometimes fall asleep.
   Yes__   No__

6. I review my notes and all the course materials periodically, throughout the semester.
   Yes__   No__

7. If I read something in English, I try to understand the meaning of words from the context and I use the dictionary only if it is absolutely necessary.
   Yes__   No__

8. For me, studying means to memorize what is in the textbook, even if I don't understand the ideas very well.
Yes__   No__

9. When I listen to a lecture, I always note down the most important ideas.
Yes__   No__

10. I am always an active participant in class.
Yes__   No__

11. If I study for long periods of time I become tired or distracted.
Yes__   No__

12. When I have to make an oral presentation, I write an outline of the main points, and I prepare it carefully, but I don't learn it word for word.
Yes__   No__

13. When I read something in English, I waste a lot of time looking up the unknown words in the dictionary.
Yes__   No__

14. When the teacher gives a lecture, I write down only what is on the board.
Yes__   No__

15. When I prepare an oral presentation, I first write it down word for word and then I learn it by heart.
Yes__   No__

16. Before a test, I always have a good night's sleep, try to feel relaxed and have a positive attitude.
Yes__   No__

If you have answered "Yes" to questions 1, 2, 6, 7, 9, 10, 12, 16, and "No" to questions 3, 4, 5, 8, 11, 13, 14, 15 you already have a positive attitude to learning and have developed some efficient studying skills. If your answers are the opposite of those mentioned, it means you need to improve your study skills in order to become a successful university student.

Finding a Good Place
Finding a good place to study is one of the basic requirements in order to be well prepared for classes, tests and exams.

? **2** *In order to see whether your room or your dorm is a good place to study, answer these questions, by checking "Yes" or "No." Read carefully the comments that accompany each question.*

1. Can you use your study place whenever you need it?
   Yes__   No__
   If you can use your place for studying whenever you need it, then it is all right. In case you have to share your study place with others, you need to agree on some rules.

2. Is your study place free from interruptions and distractions?
   Yes__   No__
   Your study place should be quiet and free from interruptions and distractions. When you have to study, you can put the "Do not disturb" sign at the door. If there are any TV sets or stereos, switch them off when you study. If you do not need your computer when studying, keep it switched off, too. If your bed is nearby and it makes you sleepy, then you'd better go to a special study room or to the library.

3. Is the table or desk in your room large enough?
   Yes__   No__
   Make sure your table or desk can accommodate all the materials you need when you study for an exam.

4. Is your study area well organized and tidy?
   Yes__   No__
   You should take care to organize your study space well, so that you can easily find the books and other study materials you need. Do not put a pile of books on your table or desk. Make sure you have a special storage space for all your materials and keep your desktop or table clear of unnecessary materials.

5. Is the in chair your study space comfortable?
   Yes__   No__
   Make sure your chair is neither too uncomfortable, nor too comfortable. In the former situation you will find it inconvenient to use it for longer periods, while in the latter case you might be tempted to fall asleep.

6. Do you have enough light in your study place?
   Yes__   No__
   Your study place should have enough natural light, so that by day you do not need any

artificial light. It is better if both natural and artificial light come from your left side, so make sure that the window and the lamp are on your left.

7. Is the temperature in your study room suitable?
Yes__   No__
The temperature in your study room should be neither too high, nor too low. Adjust it to what is suitable for both your body and mind.

Managing Time

As a university student, it is very important to manage your time well, i.e., to allot proper periods of time for all the activities you are involved in. Without a study schedule or an action plan, many of your assignments will not be finished or will be skipped off altogether.

3 *Many students tell their teachers "I didn't have time" when asked why they haven't read a certain book or why they haven't written their homework or handed in their report.*

Have **you** *ever used "I didn't have time" as an excuse for not doing your assignments? Do you* **really** *think you didn't have time to complete your assignment? Was there any other reason that made it difficult for you to complete your homework, such as* **procrastination***, i.e. putting off until it was too late what you were supposed to do?*

Discuss your answers to these questions with a partner.

Some students put off study to do something else (surf the Internet, play computer games, watch TV, go shopping, practice sports, go to the gym, etc) and then it is too late for them to finish their assignments and prepare for their courses. Their grades will be considerably lower or they may even fail to pass the exam. That is why managing your time well represents one of the keys to success as a university student.

Where Does Your Time Go?

4 *1.   In order to realize where your time goes, complete the following chart with what you did yesterday (if yesterday was weekend, complete the chart with what you did last Friday). Include all your activities from the time you woke up until you went to bed. Be as detailed and as honest as possible.*

Use of Time Chart

Time	Activities
7:00-7:30	
7:30-8:00	
8:00-9:00	
9:00-10:00	

2. Now have a look at your completed chart. Can you find any periods of 'wasted' time, which cannot be accounted for?

Principles of Planning

If you can examine your time charts for a whole week, you might be surprised at the amount of time that cannot be accounted for. This is generally time you have wasted. 'Wasted' time will no longer be a problem if you have a clear daily schedule prepared in advance. Each evening you can prepare your schedule for the following day. While planning your time, keep in mind these tips:

- Write your class timetable.
- Make a list of all your activities for each day of the week and allot each of these activities a specific amount of time (classes, sleep, meals, sports you practice, student associations and clubs, regular doctor appointments, part time job, etc).

- Plan for emergencies and unexpected events. Include some free periods which can be used to make up for study time lost because of some unexpected event.
- Write down important dates (for quizzes, oral or written reports, tests, exams, competitions).
- Plan your study time blocks. The usual study time block is 50 minutes, followed by a 10 minute break. How much time can **you** study without feeling tired or restless?
- Plan a study session after each class. If you review your course immediately after the class, while everything is fresh in your mind, it will be easier for you to prepare for your exams. If this is not possible, plan a study session for all the classes you had during the day in the afternoon or in the evening. Some freshmen think that university students do not have to study until the midterm and final exams are near. This is a false assumption and if you put off studying until the exam period, your results will be much lower than what you expected.
- Allot study time to review courses and other materials before classes. It is important to have everything fresh in your mind before starting each class.
- Plan your study time periods taking into account your study habits.

? **5** *Depending on their study/work habits people are generally divided into two main classes:*
   a. ***Early birds*** *are people who usually get up at 5 or 6 a.m. and study/work better very early in the morning, even before having breakfast.*
   b. ***Night owls*** *are the exact opposite. They are people who prefer to study/work late in the evening and at night and go to bed after 1 or 2 a.m.*
Are you an early bird or a night owl?

If you are an early bird, include your study periods early in the morning; if you belong to the latter category, place your study periods in the evening, usually after dinner.
- Be consistent. Plan to study the same subjects at the same time on the same day(s). This will help you be mentally prepared to study the respective subject and it will help you concentrate more easily.

The Daily Schedule
There are several formats you can use for your daily schedule:

1. **The Hour by Hour Timetable**
   If you use this format, you should include all the activities you perform during a day from the moment you get up until you go to bed at night.

? 6 *Use the table below to plan your activities for next Monday. Make your timetable as detailed as possible.*

Time	Activities

2. **Activities Schedule**

   Another way is to allot a certain chunk of time for each specific daily activity (classes, meals, etc) and see how much free time you still have by subtracting from 24 hours the total number of hours allotted for your various activities on a particular day.

No of hours	Activity
	Classes
	Studying (outside class)
	Student association, student clubs
	Sleeping
	Eating
	Exercise (sports)
	Work (part time job)
	Transportation (to/from university, etc)
	Personal care

24 hours

	Chores/Family commitments
	Relaxing (TV, video)
	Shopping
	Socializing/Entertainment
	Other

7 *Use the diagram above to plan your activities for next Tuesday.*

The Weekly Schedule
Starting from your daily schedule, you can create a weekly schedule.

1. If you prefer the *use-of-time* chart, your weekly schedule will look like the one below:

Time	Mon	Tues	Wed	Thu	Fri	Sat	Sun
7: 00							
7: 30							

8 *Use this schedule to plan all your activities for next week.*

Tips

- Start your schedule with the time you get up.
- Then enter your mandatory activities (classes, meals, etc).
- Insert after school and evening activities.
- Look at the empty slots you may use for studying.

2. If you prefer to plan the amount of time for *each type of activity*, you can use the following chart:

Daily activities	No of hours						
	Mon	**Tues**	**Wed**	**Thu**	**Fri**	**Sat**	**Sun**
Classes							
Studying (outside class)							
Student association, student clubs							
Sleeping							
Eating							
Exercise (sports)							
Work (part time job)							
Transportation (to/from university, etc)							
Personal care							
Chores/Family commitments							
Relaxing (TV, video)							
Shopping							
Socializing/Entertainment (with friends)							
Other							
Total							
Hours left * (24 –Total)							

* Subtract from 24 hours the total time spent on various activities and you will see how much free time is available for each day.

9 *Use the chart above to determine how much time you are going to allot to each of these activities next week.*

The Semester Schedule

Besides your short term daily and weekly schedule, you should also devise a semester schedule for important events, such as quizzes, assignment and term paper deadlines, midterm and final exam periods, sports events, student association and club meetings, etc. You can do this by inserting such dates on a semester chart.

Important dates
Academic Year_____
Semester _____

Week	1	2	3	4	5	6	7	8	9	10	11	12	13	14	15	16	17	18
Midterm exams									√									
Final exams																		√
Quizzes																		
Festivals																		

10 *Fill in the table above with the important events and dates throughout this semester. Add as many events as you think fit. Place each event in the proper week box.*

Learning Styles

As a university student, you need to take responsibility for your own learning. In order to do this and be a successful learner, however, you need to know more about your own learning style.

11 *The following quiz will help you build your own profile as a learner. For each question, circle only **one** letter (a, b or c).*

    1. I learn best
       a. when I listen to a lecture or a discussion
       b. when I actively participate and do or make something by myself (e.g. act, dance, perform an experiment, etc.)

    c. when I take detailed notes and read from a book with many pictures, diagrams or charts

2. When I listen to music, I generally
    a. hum or sing
    b. dance, move with the music or tap my feet
    c. usually close my eyes and see things that go with the music

3. When I read a book, I prefer
    a. a book with a lot of conversation (play, mystery book)
    b. a book in which I have to solve problems or answer questions
    c. a book with many illustrations, cartoons or diagrams (e.g. comics, travel book, etc)

4. If I go to a party or to a meeting and meet new people, the next day I generally remember
    a. names and discussions, but not faces
    b. what I did
    c. faces, but not names

5. In my spare time I prefer to
    a. listen to music
    b. practice sports, go to the gym or have a walk
    c. watch a movie, visit an art exhibition or view an art album

6. When I speak with someone, I prefer to
    a. speak on the phone rather than have a face-to-face conversation
    b. speak to a person while walking or participating in an activity (eating together, solving a problem)
    c. have a direct, face-to-face conversation

7. When I buy a new electronic device (a computer, a video camera, etc) and don't know how to use it, I prefer to
    a. ask someone to explain to me how to use it
    b. try to figure out by myself how to use it by trial and error
    c. look at the pictures and diagrams in the manual or software that accompanies the product

8. When I visit a new place I prefer to
    a. find a map and follow my route according to the map
    b. have a guide who can give me the necessary explanations
    c. find my way all by myself, without a map or a guide

9. When I am happy I generally
    a. shout with joy
    b. jump for joy or hug someone
    c. smile or grin

10. When I have to retell a story in class I prefer to
    a. tell it orally
    b. act it out
    c. write it down

11. When I see a word (e.g. "food") I
    a. pronounce the word silently
    b. feel the taste of a particular food in my mouth
    c. have a mental picture of a specific food I like

How many a's, b's and c's do you have? Which letter appears more often in your answers?
    a._____
    b._____
    c._____

Here is the key to the quiz:
More a's = auditory learner
More b's = kinesthetic/tactile learner
More c's = visual learner

?12 *Below you will find a brief characterization of each type. After reading it, try to guess the learning type your deskmate belongs to.*

Auditory Learners
Verbs: hear, listen
- Identify sounds and words related to an experience
- sit where they can hear the teacher well
- have good auditory skills
- are elegant, convincing speakers
- possess a special ability in handling words
- learn best when listening to lectures, discussions or debates
- can interpret underlying meaning by listening to tone, pitch, and various vocal nuances

- when reading a text, they prefer to read it aloud in order to fully understand it
- sometimes hum or talk to themselves

Careers: lawyers, politicians, writers, journalists, translators, interpreters, teachers.

Tactile Learners

Verbs: do, move, touch

- study best through a 'hands on' approach, (by *doing* things)
- sit near the door or somewhere they can get up and move around quickly
- are always on the move and find it difficult to sit still for a long period of time
- take frequent breaks
- are characterized by very good eye-hand coordination
- are very good at practical activities and sports
- enjoy going on field trips
- enjoy tasks in which they manipulate materials
- remember what was done, but forget what was said or seen

Careers: sports, crafts, acting, dancing, cooking, engineering.

Visual Learners

Verbs: see, view, watch

- prefer to sit in the front desks to view the teacher, his facial expressions, gestures and movements
- often close their eyes to visualize or remember something
- learn best from visual material - pictures, diagrams, charts, tables
- when listening to a lecture, they remember better if they take detailed notes
- remember faces, but forget names quite easily

Careers: architects, visual artists, sculptors, interior designers, engineers.

These types are rarely pure. We generally have mixed characteristics. However, one type is usually dominant.

? **13** *Work in pairs. Tell your partner what type of learner you think he/she belongs to. Then compare your answer with the results of his/her quiz. Are they the same or different?*

STUDY AIDS

Definition: What?
Study aids are those materials that can help you in your study.

? **1** *Work with a partner. Make a list of as many study aids as you can think of. You can write them in the space provided below.*

textbooks,_____

_____

_____

_____

_____

_____

_____

? **2** *In the list above, tick the aids* ***you*** *use when studying. Compare with a partner.*

The Textbook
The study aids that help you the most are, no doubt, your textbooks or coursebooks. They contain most of the information that you are expected to know about a certain subject. This information is organized in a reader friendly manner, so that what you need to learn stands out:

- Academic textbooks are structured in units, lessons or chapters, which have titles and/or numbers, i.e. **Unit/Chapter/Lesson 1** or **Study Aids**.
- The main ideas are usually placed at the beginning of each chapter or section.
- The main points usually appear in the form of headings.

- The key concepts and words are highlighted by means of typographical features:
  - bigger size of print;
  - color;
  - **bold letters**;
  - *italics*;
  - underlined words
- Lists are introduced by numbers (1, 2), letters (a, b) or bullets (•)
- Many academic textbooks have a summary at the end of each chapter and some also include a list of keywords.

As a university student, you are surrounded by many textbooks. However different from the point of view of content they may be, most academic books have some features in common. If you become familiar with these features and if you know how to use them, it will be much easier for you to find your way through the "forest" of information contained in your textbooks.

? **3** *1. Have a look at this textbook and other textbooks that you currently use this academic year. Complete the following table with the name of these textbooks. If a textbook displays the features in the left column, check (√) the appropriate box and specify where this part is located; if it doesn't have a certain feature, leave that box empty.*

Name / Features	Academic Study Skills				
Title page					
Author(s)					
Year of publication					
Publisher					
Table of contents					
Preface					
Activities, tasks, exercises					
Pictures, charts, tables or maps					
Appendices					
Bibliography (References)					
Index					
Glossary (list of special terms)					

2. Use the empty boxes at the bottom of the column on the left to insert other features that were not listed here.

? **4** *Work in groups of three or four. In your groups, discuss what features most of the textbooks in the table have in common. Where are these parts generally placed?*

Title Page

? **5** *Look at the title page and at the back of the title page for this course. Which of the elements below does it display? Check (√) the appropriate box.*

	Yes	No
title of book		
subtitle		
author(s)		
publisher		
place of publication		
year of publication		
ISBN		

ISBN means *International Standard Book Number*. It is a unique commercial book identifier, assigned to each book title, as well as to each edition and variation of a certain book. It consists of a number of digits made up of four or five parts, which are separated by hyphens or spaces:
- a group identifier (group of countries that share a language);
- the publisher code;
- the item number;
- a check digit.

Table of Contents

The *Table of contents* or simply *Contents* is a list of the parts, chapters or sections in a book or document, organized in the order in which they appear.

? **6** *Have a look at the Table of contents below. Mark the following statements T (true) or F (false).*

1. _____If you are interested in a comparison between dramatic discourse and everyday discourse you should read section 2.3.
2. _____There are *Notes and References* for each chapter.
3. _____Chapter 8 includes *Activities*, but Chapter 2 doesn't.
4. _____Chapter 7 discusses four main types of deixis: person deixis, time deixis, place deixis and discourse deixis.
5. _____The *Index* comes before the *Appendices*.
6. _____The book includes *Notes and References*, as well as a *Bibliography*.

CONTENTS

Foreword 7

1. Theatre and Life
1.1. Real and Theatrical Communication 9
1.2. Theatrical Codes 13
1.3. The Six Functions in the Theatre 14
1.4. Space 15
1.5. Time 17
1.6. Kinesic Components 18
Notes and References 20

2. Prolegomena to Discourse Analysis
2.1. Towards a Definition of Discourse 21
2.2. Dramatic and Everyday Discourse 22
2.3. Dramatic and Theatrical Discourse 24
  2.3.1. The Double Dramatic Enunciation 26
  2.3.2. Global and Individual Discourse 28
  2.3.3. Principal and Secondary Discourse 29
Notes and References 30

3. Speech Acts
3.1. A Historical View 32
3.2. A Taxonomy of Illocutionary Acts 35
3.3. Models for Analysis 37
3.4. Activities 45
Notes and References 47

4. Strategies of Discourse
4.1. A Taxonomy of Discourse Strategies 48
4.2. World 54
4.3 Face 56
4.4. Turn-Taking 57

4.5. Dramatic Worlds   58
4.6. Model for Analysis   62
4.7. Activities   62
Notes and References   65

5. Conversational Implicature
5.1. The Cooperative Principle   67
5.2. Types of Implicatures   69
5.3. Conversational Implicature and the Politeness Principle   71
5.4. Figurative Speech Acts and Conversational Implicature   73
5.5. Models for Analysis   76
5.6. Activities   84
Notes and References   86

6. Presupposition
6.1. Defining the Concept   88
6.2. Presupposition Triggers   92
6.3. Properties   93
6.4. The Theatre and Its Presuppositions   94
6.5. Models for Analysis   96
6.6. Activities   101
Notes and References   102

7. Context and Deixis
7.1. The Context-of-Utterance   103
7.2. Deixis   105
    7.2.1. Person Deixis   107
    7.2.2. Time Deixis   109
    7.2.3. Place Deixis   114
    7.2.4. Social Deixis   116
    7.2.5. Discourse Deixis   118
7.3. Anaphora and Deixis   121
7.4. Deixis and Dramatic Discourse   124
7.5. Models for Analysis   127
7.6. Activities   134
Notes and References   136

8. Modality
8.1. The Concept of Modality   139
8.2. Modal Notions and Possible Worlds   141
8.3. Epistemic Modality   142
8.4. Deontic Modality   144
8.5. Propositional Attitudes in Drama   148
8.6. Models for Analysis   149
8.7. Activities   152
Notes and References   155

9. Dramatic Dialogue
9.1. Defining the Concept   156
9.2. Monologue, Soliloquy, Aside   159

9.3. Models for Analysis	167
9.4. Activities	172
Notes and References	174
Appendices	176
Selected Bibliography	195
Index	200

The *Table of contents* can help you decide whether a book has the information you need, and if it does, it tells you where this information is located. This is very helpful, because you do not need to browse through the whole book to look for the information you need.

? **7** *Suppose you are going to write a paper on drama. Scan once again the Table of contents above to see whether you are likely to find the following information in the book the contents pages are taken from. If your answer is yes, say where it is located.*

Information about	Yes/No	Page
space and time in drama		
English drama in the 19th century		
Shakespeare's tragedies		
dramatic dialogue and monologue		
distinctions between drama and fiction		
famous American dramatists		

Footnotes
Some books and articles use footnotes to introduce the works cited on a certain page or to give more details and explanations about ideas or concepts discussed. Footnotes are inserted at the bottom of the page and are numbered using Arabic numerals.

End-of-Chapter Information and Exercises
Many textbooks include various materials at the end of each chapter: a summary of the main points, a list of keywords, various questions, exercises and activities related to the information presented in the chapter. They are valuable materials and help you better understand and review the information presented.

Illustration:
End-of-Chapter Summary

Starting from the assumption that the writer's sense of the audience influences to a great extent the content and the language of any piece of writing, this chapter has been devoted to *techniques for creating common ground*. It started with a definition of *common ground*, understood as a base of shared experience created between writer and reader. Then it presented and analyzed two main sets of techniques: those which are related to the writer's experience and reading (*narration* or *anecdote*, *quotation*, *summary* and *description*) and those which appeal to the reader's experience (*referring to the reader's experiences*, *referring to public knowledge*, *creating an analogy*). Last, but not least, the chapter discussed *tone*, the writer's general attitude toward the reader and topic and its importance in achieving successful communication.

Keywords

analogy	quotation
anecdote	reader's experience
common ground	summary
description	tone
public knowledge	writer's experience

Pictures, Charts, Diagrams and Maps
These visual materials accompany and reinforce written materials, presenting various ideas, concepts or results in a synthetic, concise and visually appealing manner. If you are a visual type of learner, charts and diagrams will prove extremely helpful in understanding new information.

Glossary
The *Glossary* is a kind of mini dictionary that appears at the end of some books, **before** the *Appendix*, *Bibliography* and the *Index*. It lists in alphabetical order various technical or specialized words that appear in the book and gives their meaning/definition and the page number where that word first appears or is defined.

Illustration:

audience	people gathered together to watch a play (p.10)
attitudinal markers	facial expressions, gestures and other paralinguistic elements that point to the speaker's attitude (p.148)
context	all the factors that determine the form, the meaning, or appropriateness of utterances (p.125)
context-of-utterance	the relationship between speaker, listener and discourse that is placed in the immediate *here- and- now* (p. 103)

Appendix (sg)/ Appendices (pl)

The *Appendix* is a section situated at the end of a book, **after** the *Glossary*, but **before** the *Bibliography* and the *Index*, which includes further data and information, sometimes presented in a visual format (pictures, charts, maps, diagrams).

Bibliography

The *Bibliography* is a list of books or articles on a certain topic situated at the end of a book or paper. Textbook bibliographies are a very good starting point for research when you have to write a report.

8 *Look at the following excerpt from a bibliography. Which of these books might you use if you were to write a paper on Theatrical communication?*

BIBLIOGRAPHY

Artaud, Antonin. *Le théatre et son double*. Paris: Gallimard, 1964.

Aston, Elaine, and George Savona. *Theatre as Sign System: A Semiotics of Text and Performance*. London: Routledge, 1991.

Austin, John L. *How to Do Things with Words*. London: Oxford University Press, 1962.

Barret, Harold. *Practical Methods in Speech*. San Francisco: Rinehard Press, 1973.

Barthes, Roland."Literature et Signification" in *Critical Essays*. Evanston: Northwestern University Press, 1964.

Bentley, Eric. *The Life of the Drama*. London: Methuen, 1964.

Benveniste, Emile. (trans.) *Problems of General Linguistics*. Miami: University of Miami Press, 1970.

Birdwhistell, Ray L. *Kinesics and Context: Essays in Body-Motion Communication*. Harmondsworth: Penguin, 1971.

Brecht, Bertold. *Brecht on Theatre*. London: Methuen, 1964.

Brook, Peter. *The Empty Space*. Harmondworth: Penguin, 1968.

Brown, Gillian and George Yule. *Discourse Analysis*. Cambridge: Cambridge University Press, 1983.

Burton, Deirdre. *Dialogue and Discourse*. London: Routledge and Kegan Paul, 1980.

9 *Have a look at the bibliography below. Answer the following questions:*

1. What is the name of the book written by J. Elliot?
2. When was Wallace's book published?

3. Where was Days' book published?
4. What is the name of the publisher of *Teachers Investigate Their Work*?
5. Who are the authors of *Focus on the Language Classroom*?
6. When was the book edited by Richards and Nunan published?
7. Which is the subtitle of Allwright and Bailey's book?
8. Which pages should you read if you are interested in Day's article?

Allwright, R. L. & Bailey, K. (1991). *Focus on the language classroom: An introduction to classroom research for language teachers*. Cambridge: Cambridge University Press.

Altrichter, H., Posch, P. & Sowekth, B. (1993). *Teachers investigate their work. An introduction to the methods of action research*. London: Routledge.

Day, R. (1990). Teacher observation in second language teacher education. In J. C. Richards & D. Nunan (Eds.), *Second language teacher education* (pp. 43-61). Cambridge: Cambridge University Press.

Elliot, J. (1991). *Action research for educational change*. Philadelphia: Open University Press.

Wallace, M. J. (1991). *Training foreign language teachers: A reflective approach*. Cambridge: Cambridge University Press.

Index

The index can also help you to check whether the information in a book is helpful for you. Situated at the back of a book, after the bibliography, the index lists in alphabetical order the topics covered in a book.

? **10** *You want to write a paper on "Theatrical communication". What entries of the index below might be helpful for your paper?*

Index

audience: 10, 11, 12, 13, 15, 16, 23, 24, 27, 32, 34, 40, 41, 42, 58, 60, 78, 80, 81, 90, 98, 116, 130, 131, 151, 158, 160, 161, 164, 165, 166, 168, 169, 170, 174

attitudinal markers: 148, 149, 150

character: 12, 13, 15, 16, 18, 19, 24, 25, 27, 28, 29, 37, 46, 59, 60, 61, 62, 76, 77, 79, 81, 99, 107, 120, 125, 126, 127, 128, 129, 131, 133, 148, 149, 150, 154, 156, 157, 158, 159, 160, 162, 163, 164, 165, 166, 168, 170, 171

codes: 9, 11, 12, 13, 14, 15, 17, 26, 82, 104, 147

non-specific codes: 14
specific codes: 14
theatrical codes: 13, 26

communication: 9, 10, 11, 12, 13, 15, 16, 20, 21, 24, 26, 27, 34, 37, 41, 62, 68, 71, 83, 91, 96, 100, 105, 156, 157, 158, 159, 160, 161, 165, 166, 169, 172
internal communication / external communication: 10, 11
process of communication: 9, 27
real and theatrical communication: 9

context: 15, 19, 22, 24, 25, 27, 28, 30, 36, 40, 42, 49, 50, 52, 53, 60, 61, 62, 69, 70, 71, 74, 75, 81, 90, 91, 92, 94, 103, 104, 105, 106, 108, 111, 113, 114, 115, 121, 123, 125, 126, 127, 128, 131, 132, 133, 134, 146, 158, 159, 167, 171
imaginary communicative context: 27
communicative context: 104, 126, 131
concrete communicative context: 27, 28
context-of-utterance: 103, 104, 105, 121, 123, 126, 128, 132, 133, 134
deixis: 25, 103, 105, 106, 107, 109, 110, 113, 114, 115, 116, 117, 118, 119, 121, 122, 123, 124, 125, 126, 131,132, 133, 134, 135, 165, 167
anaphora: 121,122, 123, 124, 132, 135, 167
authorised speakers: 116
coding time: 106,109, 156
deictic centres: 106, 108
deictic simultaneity: 137
discourse deixis: 107, 118, 119, 122, 123, 131, 132, 133, 135, 165
~and dramatic discourse: 124
participant roles: 107
person deixis: 106, 107, 131,134, 167
place deixis: 107, 114, 124, 135
proximal / distal: 107, 114, 123,126, 127, 128, 130
receiving time: 107, 109, 156, 157
roles: 13, 28, 42, 50, 104, 105, 106, 107, 108, 109, 117, 118, 124, 126, 127, 132, 156, 171
social deixis: 107, 116, 117
social roles: 104, 117, 171
social status: 117,   118, 128, 129, 130, 150, 168
tenselessness: 112
time deixis: 106, 107, 109, 110, 113, 115
timelessness: 112

dialogue: 15, 17, 21, 23, 25, 27, 28, 29, 63, 85, 102, 124, 127, 129, 135, 156, 157, 158, 159, 160, 162, 163, 164, 165, 166, 167, 172
aside: 159, 165, 166
dramatic dialogue: 23, 156, 157, 158, 167
monologue: 21, 24, 29, 44, 49, 159, 160, 162, 164, 166
planned / unplanned dialogue: 156, 157
real / fictional dialogue: 156, 157, 158
soliloquy: 159, 162, 163, 164
didascalia: 17, 29, 30, 166
discourse: 13, 15, 18, 19, 21, 22, 23, 24, 25, 26, 27, 28, 29, 30, 32, 36, 37, 41, 42, 48, 49, 50, 51, 52, 53, 57, 61, 70, 80, 81, 82, 90, 92, 94, 95, 97, 99, 104, 106, 107, 108, 118, 119, 120, 121, 122, 123, 124, 125, 126, 127, 128, 129, 130, 131, 132, 133, 134, 135, 137, 141, 150, 151, 156, 157, 158, 159, 160, 161, 162, 163, 165, 166, 167, 168, 169, 171, 172, 174
dramatic discourse: 15, 22, 23, 24, 25, 26, 27, 28, 29, 36, 37, 95, 124,125, 126, 127, 158,163, 166
everyday discourse: 22, 23, 141
global discourse / individual discourse: 28, 29
principal discourse / secondary discourse: 29
reporting discourse / reported discourse: 27
script / performance: 26
theatrical discourse: 24, 25, 26, 94, 95, 127

dramatis personae: 27, 30, 60, 96, 102, 126, 148, 164

face: 56, 72, 82,83
public face / real face: 56

felicity conditions: 46, 91, 95, 143
essential condition: 34, 40, 41, 44
preparatory conditions: 34, 40
propositional content conditions: 34

functions: 14, 15, 19, 22, 27, 51, 52, 88, 91, 103, 104, 105, 113, 114, 115, 117, 120, 121, 122, 123, 124, 126, 127, 130, 131, 133, 134, 146, 148, 162, 165, 168, 169, 170
~of language: 15
~of discourse deictics: 105 - 135

hearer: 23, 25, 28, 33, 34, 35, 36, 49, 50, 51, 52, 53, 55, 69, 70, 72, 76, 81, 91, 108, 121, 156

illocutionary act(s): 33, 34, 35, 36, 37, 39, 43, 44, 72, 73, 126, 143
assertives: 35, 36, 39, 41, 43, 44, 73, 77, 80, 98, 149, 168
commissives: 35, 38, 39, 40, 43, 44, 45, 82
declaratives: 36, 38, 94, 147, 167
directives: 27, 35, 36, 39, 40, 41, 42, 43, 44, 72, 82, 100, 144, 145, 146, 147, 166
expressives: 19, 35, 36, 39, 44

illocutionary markers: 126

implicature: 25, 67, 69, 70, 71, 73, 76, 77, 80, 81, 83, 85, 90, 93
conventional implicature: 70
conversational implicature: 25, 67, 69, 70, 71, 73, 76, 80, 81, 85, 90

interaction: 10, 12, 21, 32, 39, 40, 48, 50, 53, 54, 55, 60, 67, 72 83, 100, 105, 121, 124, 128, 133, 134, 146, 156, 158, 159, 160, 166

kinesics: 18, 19, 26, 29, 125, 126, 131, 166

listener: 34, 38, 39, 41, 69, 104, 105, 129, 127, 158, 159, 160, 170

locutionary act(s): 33

maxims (of conversation): 67, 68, 69, 70, 71, 72, 73, 74, 75, 76, 77, 78, 79, 80, 81, 82, 83, 84, 85
cooperative principle: 67, 69, 70, 71, 72,76, 84, 85
Grice's maxims: 68, 85
Lakoff's maxims: 68

The Blurb

The blurb or back cover may contain information about the structure and characteristic features of a textbook. It can also give some details about the author(s) and about the target audience. It usually includes the ISBN. In the case of modern fiction, the blurb usually contains clippings of praiseworthy reviews taken from various newspapers or magazines.

?11 *Look at the blurbs of three textbooks you currently use. What kind of information can you find in them? Complete the table below:*

Information			
about the author(s)			
about the target audience			
about the book			
clippings from reviews			
other (specify)			

?12 *Match each part of a book with the information it contains. Sometimes more than one answer is possible.*

1.__ title page	a. alphabetical list of specialized words with their meaning and the page where they appear
2.__ back of title page	b. alphabetical list of topics covered in a book
3.__ table of contents	c. title, author and publisher
4.__ preface	d. information about the book and the author
5.__ glossary	e. list of books and articles on a certain topic
6.__ appendix	f. publisher, year of publication
7.__ bibliography	g. ISBN
8.__ index	h. general presentation of the book, sometimes made by the author
9.__ blurb (back cover)	i. topics, chapters or sections covered in a book
	j. additional material and data placed at the end of a book or article

Reference Books

Reference books are usually found in a special section of a library and as a rule they cannot be taken at home. Such books contain a variety of statistical data, bibliographic information, facts, maps, and other materials. You should think of reference books as tools that may help you a lot when you need to make an oral or a written presentation. Examples of reference books are: almanacs, atlases, bibliographies, dictionaries, directories, encyclopedias.

? 13 *Match each type of reference material with the information it provides. If necessary, visit the library to find out more.*

1.__ almanac	a. book in which words related in meaning are grouped together
2.__ atlas	b. gives information on books and other materials
3.__ bibliography	c. lists alphabetically names of persons and organizations with information about how to contact them
4.__ dictionary	d. gives comprehensive information on all or specialized fields of knowledge
5.__ directory	e. an annually published book that includes statistical information
6.__ encyclopedia	f. book that contains maps and geographical information
7.__ thesaurus (sg) thesauruses/thesauri (pl)	g. book that contains alphabetically ordered words, with explanations of their meaning

The Dictionary

? 14 *Do you have a dictionary? If "yes", is it an electronic or a paper dictionary? Does it include words in only one language or in more languages?*

Dictionaries are alphabetical lists of words or entries. In the 'Reference' section of a library you can find various types of dictionaries:

- language dictionaries
- biographical dictionaries
- subject dictionaries, such as dictionaries of art, birds, business, geography, history, music, etc

Language dictionaries are among the most common dictionaries. From the point of view of the number of languages catered for, they can be classified into three main groups:

1. Monolingual dictionaries. Such dictionaries list words in a specific language, accompanied by pronunciation, definition, usage, etymology.
2. Bilingual dictionaries. These dictionaries contain alphabetical lists of words in one language with their translations in another language.
3. Multilingual dictionaries. These dictionaries give alphabetical lists of words in one language with their translation in several other languages.

Dictionaries can be printed on paper, can be consulted on a CD-ROM or online.

? 15 *Complete each column in the table below with at least 3 examples of language dictionaries. If necessary, go to the library or check the Internet.*

Monolingual dictionaries	Bilingual dictionaries	Multilingual dictionaries

Dictionaries are necessary tools for any high school or college student. They are particularly useful to those who study in depth their own language or a foreign language. Why are they so useful?

- **Dictionaries help you to build up and increase your vocabulary**. Your number one use of a dictionary is to find out the meaning of new words. At the same time, the dictionary will also help you to find additional meanings for the words you already know, thus increasing your vocabulary. The dictionary can also help you understand how a word changes its meaning when we add a prefix or a suffix.

- **Dictionaries can help you with your grammar.** The dictionary will tell you whether a word is a noun, adjective, adverb, pronoun or verb or another part of speech. It will also give the plural of certain nouns (irregular plurals, foreign plurals), as well as the three basic forms of irregular verbs.
- **Dictionaries can help you to use new words.** A dictionary gives examples in context with various meanings of one and the same word. This will help you better understand the meaning and use of words in different contexts.

In spite of these benefits, do not overuse your dictionary. When you come across new words in a text, try to guess their meaning from context. Then you can check whether your guess was correct by looking the word up in a dictionary.

The Thesaurus

A thesaurus is a reference book that includes groups of synonyms or antonyms with explanations about differences in meaning and examples. Using a thesaurus will make your text look more lively and interesting and will help you avoid repeating the same word over and over again.

?16 *Read the following sentences. Use a thesaurus to replace the words in bold with synonyms:*

1. In front of the big house there was a **big** tree which was knocked over by a **big** storm.
2. The old man was sitting in an **old** armchair on the porch of his **old** house, thinking of the **old** times.
3. The two men were **going down** the hill, following a third man who was **going** towards a small cottage which could be seen at a distance.

Encyclopedias

Encyclopedias are works that contain entries arranged in alphabetical order that give you information about various subjects. They are concerned with the *who, what, where, when, how* and *why* of things, processes, phenomena. Sometimes encyclopedias come in several volumes, with each volume including entries that cover several letters of the alphabet.

From the point of view of the information included, encyclopedias fall roughly into two main groups:

1. **General encyclopedias.** These encyclopedias include entries from all kinds of areas. The best known general encyclopedia is probably *Encyclopaedia Britannica*, which covers almost any topic one can think of.

2. **Specialized encyclopedias.** These encyclopedias cover one area of knowledge or one field, such as science, technology, modern art, medicine, pop and rock music, etc.

From the point of view of the medium or channel, we can distinguish **printed encyclopedias** and **on-line encyclopedias.** One of the best known and most widely used on-line encyclopedias is probably *Wilkipedia*.

A word of warning! Whenever you need to search for **reliable** information about a certain subject, i.e. when you need information for your graduation paper or for your dissertation, it is better to use a printed encyclopedia. The information there has been written by a group of experts and has been checked thoroughly.

Atlases

If you want to know the distance from Taipei to Kaohsiung, the highest mountain in Europe or the deepest ocean in the world, the reference book you need is an atlas. Atlases usually contain maps, charts, diagrams and tables that give you information about cities, countries, continents, mountains, plateaus, plains, rivers, seas and oceans. They also show the distribution of economic resources, population, industry, types of climate, roads. The maps included in atlases may be of various types: *physical maps* show the distribution of different forms of relief; *economic maps* present the distribution of agriculture, industry branches and transportation systems; *tourist maps* tell you about the most important places to visit, etc. The index at the end will help you locate the specific information you are looking for.

17 *Go to the library and look for an atlas of your country. Find information about:*

1. your county: name, geographical position, surface, population, most important city
2. your hometown: name, geographical position, population
3. relief of your home area: mountains, plains, rivers, lakes, sea, ocean, etc
4. wildlife and plants in your home area
5. economic features of your home town: farm production, industry, transportation
6. tourist attractions in your home town: natural scenery, museums, memorial houses, old buildings, temples/churches, theme parks, etc

18 *Use this information to write a text of about 300 words entitled "My Hometown". The text should give information and also persuade tourists to visit your hometown. Cover all the six points mentioned above.*

Almanacs. Almanacs are reference books that are published each year. They include all kinds of information, such as important dates and events, facts about government, history, geography, sports and weather. So, if you want to know America's export-import balance last year or how many barrels of oil were produced in Saudi Arabia last year, use an almanac.

Some Words of Caution

When using reference books, especially encyclopedias, atlases and almanacs, you should try to find the latest edition, because some information in these books, such as maps, facts, statistical information can be outdated. So check the copyright date at the back of the title page. The most recent date on the copyright page tells you when the volume was published. On the other hand, it is advisable to check for the same information in several reference books, in order to be sure you get reliable information.

Periodicals

Beside books the library offers you other valuable sources of information, roughly grouped under the heading *periodicals*:

- newspapers
- magazines
- journals

These sources are very useful if you need information that is current or focused on a specific topic. A *newspaper* is printed daily (sometimes weekly) on lower cost paper and contains hot local, domestic and international news, various kinds of general information (political, economic, cultural, etc) and advertising. A *magazine* is a periodical publication issued weekly, bimonthly, monthly, or quarterly and printed in colors on good quality paper that can present information of general or more specific interest in a language that is usually accessible to everyone. *Journals* are academic or professional periodicals that include research articles in specific domains. At the end they provide a bibliography with the works that have been cited. Their style is different from that of newspapers and magazines: journals use a scientific, objective style that tries to erase the traces of the author from the text and to highlight the results obtained. Journal articles are more difficult to read and be understood by a layperson because they use specific language called *jargon*, i.e., terms and concepts that are specific to professionals in a certain field. Thus, a medical journal will use medical jargon; a journal of linguistics will use a different kind of jargon, a.s.o.

?19 *Answer the following questions:*

1. Give the name of three English or American newspapers.

2. Give the name of three newspapers issued in your country which are written in English.

3. Do you read any newspapers in English? If yes, are they English/American or are they printed in your country? How often do you read them? Do you read all the articles or only some? Which rubrics are your favourites?

4. Can you name three English or American magazines?

5. Do you read any magazines in English? Do you read them on a regular basis or just from time to time? Which is your favourite?

6. In the table below, write the name of three English or American journals in the following fields that can be found in your university library: literature, linguistics, English language teaching (ELT) and culture.

Literature	Linguistics	English Language Teaching	Culture

? **20** *Look at these statements. Which apply to textbooks, which apply to encyclopedias, which apply to journals, and which are true about all these categories? Check (√) the appropriate box(es). Be ready to defend your choices.*

	Textbooks	Encyclopedias	Journals
a detailed analysis of a topic			
up-to-date information on a topic			
detailed reports on research and findings			
bibliography of related information			
general information on a subject			
use of jargon			
a brief explanation or summary of an idea			
critical views on a specific issue			
review of the research and ideas on a specific topic			

Other Study Aids
The Computer

The computer in your home or dorm is much more than an object on which you can play DVDs or video games. It is an invaluable aid that can help you find information and can reduce your study time. There are many software programs that can help you improve your English language skills. Most textbooks are accompanied by CDs or DVDs with self-study materials. On the other hand, important publishers have websites that contain, among other things, supplementary materials and exercises for the textbooks they publish. If you do not have a printed dictionary, you can use your computer to find various monolingual and bilingual on-line dictionaries. You can also browse the Internet to find different electronic newspapers, magazines or journals.

? **21** *How do you use your computer in your study? Tick what is true about you.*

I use the computer to
- find more information on various subjects I am studying
- find the meaning of unknown words
- do supplementary exercises
- watch English and American movies
- read online newspapers and magazines in English
- read English and American literature available on the Internet
- read English journals online
- write messages and c-mails in English
- other uses (please specify)

Radio and Television

Radio and television can also help you find ideas and information that may be used for your oral or written reports. They can also improve your English language skills.

? **22** *Do you watch any TV channels in English? Which of the following do you watch? How many hours a week do you watch each of them? Complete the following table:*

Channel	How Often?
CNN	
Discovery	
National Geographic	

Animal Planet	
Travel and Living	
HBO	
AXN	
Cinemax	
Star Movies	
E-movies	
Hollywood	
Other (please specify)	

NOTE-TAKING

Definition: What?

What means to take notes?

 **1** *Complete the following definition:*

Note-taking means writing_____

_____

Now work in a group. In your group, read your definition and listen to the ones of the other group members. Agree upon the best definition to be read to the whole class.

Purpose: Why?

In everyday life, we take notes (while listening to other people speaking or while reading books or articles) for various reasons.

- A doctor, for example, may take notes while listening to a patient speaking about his/her symptoms in order to determine the patient's diagnosis. The same doctor may make notes while reading an article in a medical journal because he is interested in the topic.

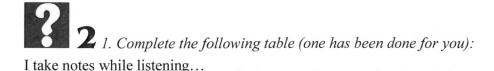 **2** *1. Complete the following table (one has been done for you):*

I take notes while listening…

Situation	Reasons
• to a lecture in class	• to help me remember (what the teacher said)

I take notes while reading…

Situation	Reasons
• a book	• to help me remember (what the author wrote)

2. Are there any similar reasons in the two tables?
3. Are there any different reasons? Why?
4. Place them under one of these headings:

Similar reasons	Different reasons

Compare your reasons with a partner. Discuss and complete your tables if necessary.

As you can see, there are similarities, but also differences between the reasons for writing notes from listening and reading, respectively.

SPA

Any piece of writing is characterized by *subject, purpose and audience.* What happens in the case of notes?

- the *subject* may vary a lot from one set of notes to another
- the *purpose* is to inform
- the *audience* or *reader* is usually the person who wrote the notes.
- notes are a *secondary type* of writing, i.e. the *source* is different from the *author of notes.* The source may be represented by a **spoken text** (a lecture, a telephone conversation, the doctor's recommendations, discussions during a student association meeting or during a department meeting etc), or by a **written text** (a book, textbook, newspaper or journal article you are reading).

Therefore

source ≠ author of notes

This means that notes are a personal kind of writing, written by **yourself** to serve **your** purpose, i.e. study for exams, use ideas from notes (while acknowledging sources) for your research, etc. This means that, broadly speaking, there are as many styles of taking notes as there are people.

Taking Notes in Class

Characteristics of Notes: How?

People take notes in different ways. There is no **right way** to take notes.

3 *How do you take notes? Think of the way you take notes in English.*

Do you use any symbols, short forms or abbreviations?

Complete this chart with what is true about you:

Abbreviations and Short Forms	Symbols

Notes are written in a **concise** manner. This means that when making notes
- we generally use **abbreviations**;
- we make use of certain **symbols**;
- we generally **omit grammatical words** such as articles, auxiliary verbs, prepositions, conjunctions.

4 *Below you can see some abbreviations and symbols used by English speakers.*

Match them with the corresponding words/phrases.

1. e.g.	a) number	9. =	i) less than
2. i.e.	b) compare with	10. ≈	j) more than
3. viz.	c) that is	11. ≠	k) equals (is the same as)
4. cf.	d) take note	12. →	l) is not the same as
5. etc.	e) for example	13. ←	m) results from
6. NB	f) and so on	14. >	n) is proportional to
7. no	g) pages	15. <	o) is approximately equal to
8. pp	h) namely	16. α	p) causes

1	2	3	4	5	6	7	8	9	10	11	12	13	14	15	16

Using abbreviations, symbols and omitting certain words or sentences will help you take notes more quickly. This is especially important when you have to **take notes from lectures**.

5 *Why do you think it is particularly important to use abbreviations and symbols when you take notes during lectures? Try to remember the last time you did that.*

In such cases writing takes place in real time. Therefore, unless the professor dictates (which is unusual), it is quite hard (if not impossible) to take notes *verbatim* (word by word). The results of such an unfortunate attempt will be blank spaces and illegible handwriting.

On the other hand, the habit of taking notes *verbatim* might turn you into an automaton: instead of thinking about the ideas in the lecture, you will be busy writing each and every word. Let us not forget that an important function of taking notes from lectures is to store the information visually, auditorily and kinesthetically (i.e. by means of movement).

Tips for Using Abbreviations

You can develop your own style for abbreviating (shortening) almost any word. Here are three techniques that can help you do that:

1. Write only the beginning of the word and omit the rest. This technique can be applied with longer words:

Word	Abbreviation
abbreviation	abbrev
information	info

2. Leave out the vowels and write only the consonants:

Word	Abbreviation
package	pkg
teacher	tchr

3. Write just the first and the last letter in the case of one-syllable words:

Word	Abbreviation
pack	pk
road	rd

Remember: Do **not** make abbreviations for each and every word! Abbreviate only the words for which you know the standard abbreviation (see exercise above) or for words you meet quite often and you can form your own style.

6 *Try to abbreviate the following words:*

writing, student, language, literature, technology, business, memorandum, university, communication, speaking, listening.

7 *Look at these two sets of notes taken during part of a lecture on **Higher Education in Britain** by two different students. Both use abbreviations and symbols, yet they are different. What makes them different?*

a) **Entry requir.**

Ss apply → interview (univ. sets requir.) → Ss know ab. standards

Weekly load

ab. ⟨ 4 main courses ⟨ 3 / 4 ⟩ contact hrs. = 16 hrs. ⟩ 20-22 hrs
2 opt. courses

Assessment ⟨ coursework (CA' s + lab) ≈ 40 - 50%
final exam ≈ 50 - 60 %

b) transparent system, i.e. - students apply for univ.

S. is invited for an interview, the univ. will set requirements and the S. will go away knowing what to do this acts as a good incentive

Ss. have ab. 4 main courses (3-4 contact hours) and 2 optional courses – so in total = 20 - 22 contact hours/week

Assessment – smt. cont. assessment testing cumulative knowledge (about 40-50 % of the final grade) and final exam will represent about 50-60%.

 8 *Which of these notes do you prefer and why? Discuss with a partner.*

The examples above point to another characteristic of notes, i.e., *layout* or the way your notes are arranged. No matter what your style is, notes should always have a **clear layout** and should be **reader-friendly**, i.e. you should be able to **understand** them if you read them after a few days, weeks or years.

Some Tips

Here are some tips that can help you to write more efficient notes during lectures:

Before Class
- check the syllabus to see what the lecture is about
- read something on the topic before class
- review your notes from previous class
- bring pens, pencils and paper/notebook

During Class
- stay focused
- listen attentively to the introduction. The introduction usually specifies two important elements: the *topic* of the lecture and the *main points*.
- listen for "signal" words or phrases, i.e. words that preface something important: "Remember that…", "Don't forget that…", "The most important point…" and start writing when you hear these words
- listen for words or phrases that are stressed and write them down
- if your teacher repeats an idea several times, you should note it down
- note down what the teacher writes on the board
- use abbreviations and symbols
- you can use bullet points, letters or numbers for main points
- if you get behind, make a mark on your paper or leave some space, but **do not** stop writing

- leave a margin on the left side of your paper. When you review your notes, you can use this space to write the main ideas

After Class
- try to complete the blank spaces in your notes, by comparing your notes with those taken by a colleague
- review your notes the same day, when ideas are still fresh
- use the left margin to write the main ideas
- in order to help you remember you can use:
  color coding
  highlighting
  <u>underlining</u>

  | boxing |

  (ringing)

- bullets
  arrows (→, ↔, ←) for linking ideas

?9 *Listen to the introduction of a lecture. Complete the following notes with the topic and main points.*

Topic: _____

Main ideas discussed by the speaker:
1. _____
2. _____

?10 *Now listen to part of the lecture and complete these notes. Use abbreviations and symbols when possible.*

Struct. of ed. syst. in UK

4 levels

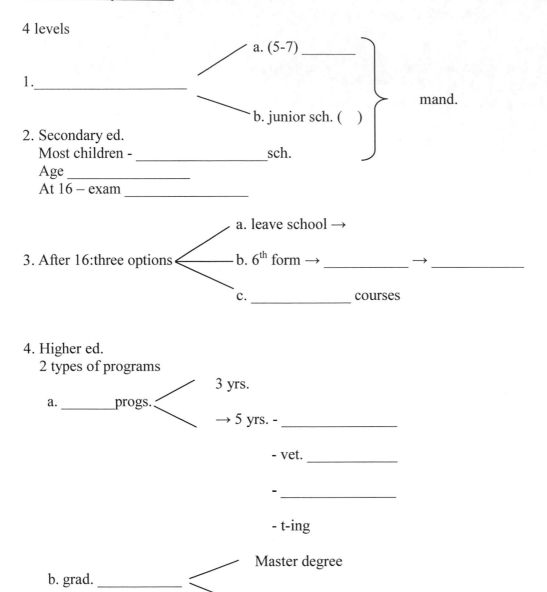

a. (5-7) _____

1. _____

b. junior sch. (   )

} mand.

2. Secondary ed.
   Most children - _____ sch.
   Age _____
   At 16 – exam _____

a. leave school →

3. After 16:three options

b. 6th form → _____ → _____

c. _____ courses

4. Higher ed.
   2 types of programs

   a. _____ progs.

   3 yrs.

   → 5 yrs. - _____

   - vet. _____

   - _____

   - t-ing

   b. grad. _____

   Master degree

   _____

Taking Notes from Reading Material

As you have already seen, notes can be taken while listening or while reading certain materials. Notes taken while listening have to be taken in **real time**; notes taken from reading material do not have such time constraints. So you can spend more time reading a book or an article, thinking and taking notes. That is why notes from reading are usually better organized than notes from listening. The way you organize your notes and the ideas you include in your notes depend on your style, purpose, and focus. As a result, there are various methods and strategies for taking and organizing notes from reading materials.

SQRW

One such strategy is called *SQRW* (Survey, Question, Read, and Write). *SQRW* is a strategy that can help you focus better on reading your textbook and take better notes from such reading materials for class or exam purposes. When using this strategy, follow these steps:

Before Reading/Writing
- Gather the essential tools: the reading matter (books, articles, etc), pens and pencils
- Find a comfortable place to work. Remember that the light source should be on your left side.

Surveying the Material (S)
Scan the material and read
- the chapter title
- the headings and subheadings
- the introduction
- the section and chapter summaries or conclusions
- any diagrams, graphs and tables

Surveying the material will familiarize you with the text and will make you feel more comfortable.

Question (Q)
- Formulate questions in your mind (you can also write them on paper) as you read. Ask questions about the title, headings and subheadings by changing them into *wh-questions*, i.e. questions that start with *who, what, why, where, when, how*.
- If a heading is formulated as a question, use this question.
- If a heading contains more than one idea, formulate a question about each idea.

 11 *Look at the following headings and subheadings. Ask questions about them:*

Headings and subheadings	Questions
Note taking: definition	
Characteristics of notes	
Taking notes in class	
Taking notes from reading material	

Read (R)
- Read attentively. Concentrate on what you are reading.
- Read the information that comes after each heading. Try to find answers to the questions you asked.
- Be flexible. If necessary, change your questions or/and add other questions as you read.

? 12 *Select the subheading "Characteristics of notes". Read the corresponding section from this book. Do you think you should change your question? Can you add any other questions?*

Write (W)
- Write each question and corresponding answer in your notebook. Give clear and concise answers to your questions.
- Read again each answer. Make sure each answer contains all the important information.

Picking out the Main Ideas
This is another method for taking notes from written sources. The main difference between this method and the previous one is that, instead of writing questions, you select the main idea of each paragraph. The steps are the following:

Before Reading/Writing
- Gather the essential tools: the reading matter (books, articles, etc), pens and pencils
- Find a comfortable place to work. Remember that the light source should be on your left side.

Surveying the Material (S)
Scan the material and read
- the chapter title
- the headings and subheadings
- the introduction
- the section and chapter summaries or conclusions
- any diagrams, graphs and tables

Picking out Main Ideas
- While reading, pick out the main ideas. Remember that each paragraph revolves around one topic or a group of related topics. The topic or main idea is generally

stated in the *topic sentence* – usually the first sentence in a paragraph. Sometimes, however, the topic sentence may not be included in certain paragraphs. In this case, you should read the paragraph attentively and express the main idea in your own words.

- Write only the main ideas in the order in which they appear. Do not include details or secondary ideas.

?13 *Below are some paragraphs that give advice on how to write a CV. Pick out the main ideas expressed in the topic sentences. Whenever necessary, express the main idea in your own words. The topic sentence in paragraph 2 has been underlined to give you an example.*

1. A handwritten CV is unacceptable, typed is better and one composed on a word processor is best. Remember, keep is short! Busy employers do not have the time to read a rambling narrative, and won't be impressed by one. They want facts: qualifications, skills and experience and should be able to see at a glance exactly what you have to offer them.

2. <u>A good CV should run to no more than two pages of A4</u>. This applies right the way up to senior management level, so those with far less experience (that means you, graduates!) should limit themselves to a single page.

3. The layout should be clear and easy on the eye. Leave wide margins on either side of the page. Use bold type for headings and bullet points for noteworthy achievements.

4. Unless you have some truly amazing and relevant experience, perhaps from a placement, it's generally best to lead with your education. Place it in chronological order, and don't use abbreviations. Writing down "Eng. Lit" instead of "English Literature", for example, will look sloppy.

5. You should always list any work experience in reverse chronology, i.e. putting the most recent position first. If you have achieved anything noteworthy at work, or had some responsibility, say so.

Organizing Your Notes

Notes can be organized in different ways, depending on your own *style* and on the *purpose* you have in mind. However, as shown above, notes should be **clear**, i.e. you should be able to **understand** them if you read them after a few days.

Annotations

One simple way of organizing your notes is to make **annotations**. The word, coming from Latin, refers to critical and explanatory notes or comments which may be added on the margins of the page when reading a book, an article etc. They may consist in isolated words or symbols or may develop into expanded comments. One advantage of making annotations is that you can *'translate'* your thoughts onto paper the moment they appear in your mind. One problem is that annotations can easily turn into **digressions**, which although sometimes very interesting, may not prove useful to your purpose. Another problem is that you cannot make annotations on the margins of a book or article you have borrowed.

However, if you can keep your annotations short and to the point, they can be used as a valuable tool for reading in a critical, active manner. On the other hand, annotations can be further on developed into expanded notes, explanations, or critical comments.

Illustration

Here are some annotations made by a student who has read part of the text giving advice on how to write a good CV.

What is required is a punchy, precise and well-presented summary of your strengths and achievements. It's a simple thing to get right, but you have to know how.	qualities of a good CV
A handwritten CV is unacceptable, typed is better and one composed on a word processor is best. Remember, keep it short! Busy employers do not have time to read a rambling narrative, and won't be impressed by one. They want facts: qualifications, skills and experience – and should be able to see at a glance exactly what you have to offer them.	**not** handwritten best word-processed short should include facts
A good CV should run to no more than two pages of A4. This applies right the way up to senior management level – so those with far less experience (that means you, graduates!) should limit themselves to a single page.	length→2A4 pp
The layout should be clear and easy on the eye. Leave wide margins on either side of the page. Use bold type for headings and bullet points for noteworthy achievements.	layout–clear wide margins bold and bullets

Linear Notes

Another way is to make **linear notes** on paper. In this case *bullets, hyphens* or other symbols can be used to introduce the main ideas. The most important words can be made prominent by *underlining* them or by using a *highlighter*.

Illustration

Here is an example of linear notes that can be taken from the text giving tips on how to write a CV.
- CV General Characteristics

- punchy
- precise
- well-presented
- includes facts   - qualif.
                        - skills
                        - exp.

- <u>Length</u>
  - short
  - 1-2 A4 pp

- <u>Layout</u>
  - clear
  - easy on the eye
  - bold - headings
  - bullets - imp. achv.

Mapping

Mapping can be used as a technique for organizing notes. Notes written in graphic form are considered to be very helpful because: a) they can be written very quickly and b) they can be recalled quite easily.

Illustration

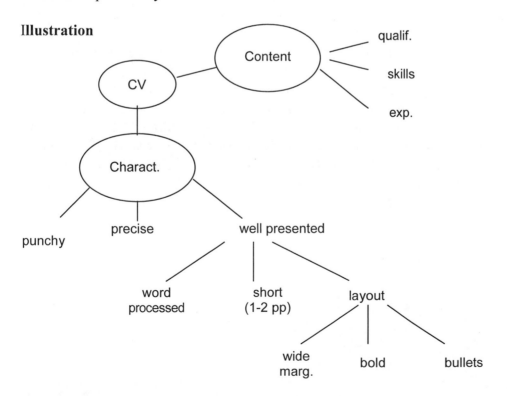

Diagrams

Sometimes, especially in the case of texts that present a classification, it is easier to take notes in the diagram format.

 14 *Read the following text and complete the classification diagram:*

The Media

Mass media have become part of our daily life. We cannot imagine our life without newspapers, magazines, radio, television or the internet. But how can we define the media and what categories belong to this big class?

The media can be defined as any medium used for transmitting mass communication messages. According to the way the message is transmitted, we can classify mass media into two groups: printed media and electronic media. ***Printed media*** include publications which, although processed electronically nowadays, are written on paper. The verb associated with them is *read*. This category includes newspapers and magazines. A newspaper is usually printed daily (sometimes weekly) on low cost paper and contains hot news, information and advertising. A magazine is a periodical publication, issued weekly, monthly, bimonthly or quarterly and printed in colors on good quality paper that presents news and information on various subjects.

Electronic media use electronic or electromagnetic energy for the audience to access content. Roughly they include three main categories: radio, television and the internet. Radio involves the transmission of audio signals which are then decoded and *listened to*. Television refers to the transmission of video signals, which are decoded by means of the proper equipment. The verb associated with TV programs is *watch*. The internet, a breakthrough in the development of mass media, is the worldwide network of computer networks that transmit data using the standard Internet Protocol. The internet often uses multimedia format, combining text, graphics, photos, films. That is why the verbs associated with the internet may be some or all of the following: *read, listen to, watch.*

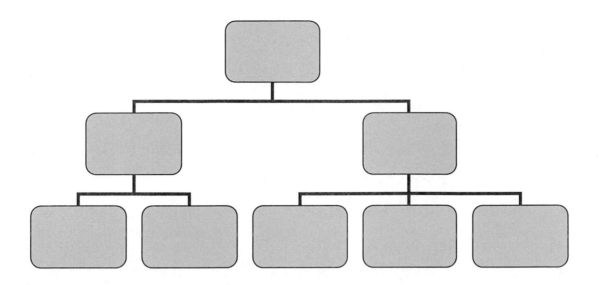

Tables

Notes from written sources can also be taken in tabulated form (in tables). A table is formed of several columns and rows in which you can insert your notes in a systematic manner.

15 *Below you can find some notes from the first part text **The Media** in tabulated form. Complete the table with information from the text:*

Printed Media

Types		Magazines
Frequency	daily/weekly	
Paper		good quality
Contents	hot news, info, advert	

SUMMARIZING

Definition: What?

A *summary* is a relatively brief, objective account in your own words of the main ideas in a text or part of a text.

Purpose: Why?

- to extract the main points from a relatively long passage
- to condense information essential to your own essay or piece of research

SPA

- The *subject* (S) is that of the material you are summarizing (a book, an article, etc.).
- The main purpose (P) of a summary is *to inform* in a concise manner. However, sometimes its secondary purpose can be that of *persuading* (e.g. persuading the reader to buy a recently published or a forthcoming novel).
- The intended *reader* may be
  - the writer of the summary himself/herself (when you write a summary in order to better remember the main ideas in an article or the plot of a novel)
  - the teacher (when you are asked to write a summary as part of your coursework)
  - any reader of a certain publication/ any internet surfer (when your summary appears in printed/ electronic media)
- Just like notes, a summary is a secondary type of writing, i.e. the ideas in the summary belong to the source material, not to the writer of the summary. Therefore, when you write a summary, you do **not** include your own ideas. Unlike notes, however, which can be made up of symbols and words (sometimes abbreviated), phrases and parts of sentences, a summary is made up of complete sentences that are connected to a certain topic.

Summarizing an Article
Characteristics of a Summary

? 1 *Read the following statements. They give some tips on what you should/ shouldn't do when writing a summary. The tips are written in italics. In each pair, one tip is correct, the other one is false. Circle the correct tip in each statement. The first one has been done for you.*

An effective summary

1. *should /* ⟨ *shouldn't* ⟩ be long.
2. should include the main ideas *in the same order in which they appeared in the original text/ in a different order from the one in the original text.*
3. *should/ shouldn't* include secondary ideas or details.
4. *should/ need not* be easy to read and understand.
5. *should/ shouldn't* use abbreviations.
6. *should/ need not* use complete sentences.
7. *should/ shouldn't* include your own thoughts about the topic.
8. *should/ shouldn't* be expressed in your own words.

? 2 *Read the following article and the summary that accompanies it. Which tips in Exercise 1 are observed by the author of the summary? Make a list and compare with a partner.*

Ecological Transport: You Can Use It, Too

How do you go to university or to work every day? Do you drive a car? Do you ride a motorbike? Do you ride a bike? Or do you just walk? If you are really concerned about your own health and the health of the environment, the best options are the last two: walking and riding a bike can keep you fit and don't pollute the environment.

Denmark is one of the leading countries to have implemented sustainable transport policy in order to promote an efficient, non polluting transport system for both the general public and industry. The implementation of the national transport policy in the 1990s as a direct result of the concern over global warming has led to the promotion of sustainable transport. Sustainable transport increases transport efficiency and provides grater mobility for the population without harming the environment. Sustainable transport policies encourage walking, cycling, and using public transport rather than personal cars or motorcycles.

Cycling, one of the most important means of eco-friendly transport is used on a wide scale in Denmark. As far as the weight of cycling in general transport is concerned, Denmark rates way ahead Germany and Austria, two other European countries with important achievements in environmentally friendly transport.

In Asia, Japan seems to be one of the countries that are highly concerned about the promotion and implementation of sustainable transport. One of Japan's major

preoccupations is the reduction of carbon emissions from vehicles, by replacing conventional oil-based fuels with hydrogen fuel. To do that, Japan will invest $11 billion in a project spanning over 28 years.

Just like Denmark, Japan has been using eco-friendly, non-motorized transportation on a wide scale. Thus, over 80% of Japanese households own at least one bike; the national average amounts to 1.42 bikes per household. The Japanese government recognized the benefits of bike travel and walking when, back in the 1970s, 37,000 miles of additional bike/ pedestrian pathways were provided for the population.

Summary

The article "Ecological Transport: You Can Use It, Too" deals with the implementation of environmentally friendly transport in Denmark and Japan, two of the countries that lead the way as far as non-polluting, sustainable transport is concerned. The author discusses first Denmark's eco-friendly transportation policy. As a result of this policy, in Denmark bicycles are used on a large scale, much more than in Germany or Austria. The article then focuses on the measures that have been taken in Japan to reduce carbon emissions. Specifically it discusses the development of non-polluting, alternative fuels, such as hydrogen and the use of non-motorized transportation, such as cycling and walking. (107 words)

By now you have probably realized that effective summaries have the following characteristics:
- They are concise, clear and reader friendly.
- They are written in complete sentences and do not use abbreviations.
- Summaries include only the main ideas in the order in which they appear in the original text.
- As a consequence, you should not include in your summary your own thoughts or ideas that are not found in the original text.
- However, a summary should be expressed in your own words. **Do not copy** phrases or sentences from the text you are summarizing.
- If you summarize an article or a chapter from a book, a one-paragraph summary is enough.
- The first sentence of a summary states the name of the article/ book, that of the author (and also the date of publication, if available), together with the main point.

- The last sentence should summarize the conclusions formulated in the source article/ book.

Analyzing and Evaluating Summaries
Devising a Checklist

In order to evaluate a summary in an objective manner, you need a checklist. This checklist is a set of criteria against which you can "measure" the quality of a text. You can create such a checklist from the characteristics above, by turning them into questions.

? **3** *Work in groups of 3 or 4. Make a checklist for evaluating summaries from the characteristics above. An example is given below. After finishing, have a whole-class discussion. Choose the best checklist.*

Checklist for Summaries

	Yes	No
1. Does the summary start with a sentence that gives the name of the article?		

? **4** *Read the article below and the three summaries that follow. Use the checklist you devised to decide which summary is the best.*

Asian Elephants at War with Humans

Asian elephants and their natural habitat are in real danger due to population growth, mass movements in search for new lodging, agricultural clearing and poorly planned extensive economic development. According to a report released by World Wide Fund (WWF), in various Asian regions elephants are being killed for their meat, hide and tusks or because they are considered a threat to the crops. Many others die in train or road collisions. Moreover, in densely populated areas situated near the elephants' forest habitat, there have been reported violent clashes between humans and Asian elephants.

Part of the land that once represented

the Asian elephants' natural habitat has been taken over by humans to be used for constructions or agriculture. According to recent estimations, about 20% of the world's population lives in or near the range of the Asian elephant. While the population in these regions increases by approximately 3% every year, the total number of Asian elephants has decreased to a total of 35,000-50,000 animals in the wild, which represents less than one tenth of the estimated number of African elephants.

The continuous population growth in these regions has resulted in the clearance of forest for human settlements and agriculture. This has decreased the elephants' natural habitat and has disrupted their traditional migration routes. Not finding enough food in their new confined surroundings, hungry elephants turned to the farmers' crops that now occupy their former habitat. This has led to violent, often fatal clashes between humans and elephants, with great losses on both sides: reports estimate that hundreds of people are killed in Asia by elephants each year and that the number of Asian elephants that are poisoned or shot by angry farmers is also on the rise.

WWF calls for all governments responsible to take urgent steps for the protection of elephants, as well as of other endangered species, such as rhinos and tigers. This can be done by enforcing sound forest use practices that comply with national and international legislation regarding biodiversity protection, by enforcing strict anti-poaching measures and by banning trade of Asian elephant products, such as tusks and hide.

Summary 1

The article shows why humans are responsible for the dramatic decrease of elephant population in Asia. Elephants are killed for their meat, tusks and hide or because they have become a threat for the population living close to them. Many also die as a result of train or road collisions. The habitat of Asian elephants has become smaller and smaller, due to the fact that part of the land that was once populated with elephants is now used for constructions or agriculture. It is estimated that about 20% of the human population live close to Asian elephants. The increasing population in these regions has led to the clearance of forests for human settlements and agriculture. This has disrupted elephants' habitat and migration routes and has led to conflicts with humans arising from the elephants' search for food in areas that used to be theirs, but are now inhabited by humans. Many elephants and people die due to such conflicts. The author urges the governments of Asian countries to implement urgent measures for the protection of elephants and other endangered species, such as rhinos and tigers. I also think elephants and other endangered species need more protection from all of us. (200 words)

Summary 2

The article named "Asian Elephants at War with Humans" urges for urgent measures to be taken in order to stop possible clashes between humans and elephants which have a as a result a continuous decrease in the number of Asian elephants. (41 words)

Summary 3

The article "Asian Elephants at War with Humans" urges the governments of Asian countries to take urgent measures for the protection of elephants. Elephants have to leave their forest habitat because forests are cleared out to form new human settlements or expand agricultural surfaces. A recent report released by World Wildlife Fund shows that many elephants are killed by people or die in traffic collisions. Their habitat has been narrowed down and their migratory routes have been disrupted by the continually growing human population. This has led to violent clashes between humans and elephants in search for food. In order to address these problems, World Wildlife Fund urges governments of Asian countries to take clear steps to protect elephants and other endangered species. (123 words)

5 *Which of the three summaries is the best? Why?*

Summary _____ is the best.

Reasons:

_____

_____

_____

_____

_____

_____

6 *Analyze the other two summaries. Use the checklist to decide what kinds of problems they have. Write down the number of each summary and its corresponding problems.*

Summary: _____
Problems:

_____

_____

_____

_____

_____

_____

Summary: _____

Problems:

_____

_____

_____

_____

_____

_____

Completing a Summary

 7 *Read the following article and complete the summary that follows:*

Left or Right?

Are you right-handed or left-handed? Studies performed in the late 1990s suggest that 7 to 10% of the world adult population is left handed and that left-handedness occurs more frequently in males than in females. While in the past, the left limbs (arms, hands, legs) had usually negative connotations, meaning something 'bad' or 'sinister', or mere 'clumsiness', recent studies published in medical journals seem to contradict this misconception, showing that left-handed people may perform better than right-handers when it comes to piloting a jet fighter or talking and driving at the same time. The results of a study published in the journal *Neuropsychology* show that left-handers are faster at processing multiple stimuli than right-handers.

Recent research conducted at the Australian National University (ANU) suggests that left-handers are able to process language using both hemispheres of the brain, while righties use primarily their left hemisphere for this purpose.

The study at ANU involved 100 subjects, out of which 80 were right-handed and 20 left-handed. The tests the subjects were involved in were meant to investigate the speed of information flow between the two hemispheres. In one of these tests, a computer display showed a single dot on either the left or the right side of a dividing line, and the subjects were asked to quickly press a button to show on which side of the line they saw the dot. The left-handed subjects proved to be faster at this task than the right-handed ones. Another test asked subjects to match up multiple letters that sometimes appeared on either side of the dividing line and at other times appeared just on one side. The results showed that the left-handed subjects were faster at matching up the letters that appeared on both sides; right-handed subjects, on the other hand, were faster at matching the letters that appeared on only one side of the line. These tests suggest that lefties are faster than righties at processing stimuli that target both hemispheres, whereas right-handed people are faster at processing stimuli that address only one side of the brain.

These findings support the observation that the connection between the two hemispheres seems to be larger and better realized in the case of left-handers. Left-handers can use more easily both brain hemispheres to respond to and manage stimuli, which means that they may be better in sports, games and other activities in which people have to face a large amount of stimuli coming from different directions at the same time or in rapid succession. This can also mean that, if due to some injury or old age, one hemisphere starts to slow down, its work may be taken over by the other one.

The article entitled (1)_____ presents the results of a study published in (2)_____ which show that (3) _____ are better able to process (4)_____ than (5)_____. Research shows that left-handed people can process language with (6)_____, while right-handed people use only (7)_____. This supports the idea that left-handers can use (8)_____to manage (9)_____, which means that they are better in (10)_____.

How to Write a One-Paragraph Summary
The steps below can help you write an effective summary of an article or a textbook chapter.

1. Prewriting
- Read the article quickly to determine the author's main point. This first reading is important because it will familiarize you with the material you are going to summarize.

2. Reading and Note-Making

- Read again the article.
- Take notes on the main points using your own words. Write down as many ideas as the number of paragraphs in the source article.

3. Writing a First Draft

- Write your first draft from your notes.
- Do not look back at the original material while you are writing it.
- Include in your summary only the author's main points.
- Do not include any minor points.
- Your draft should contain:
  - A topic sentence (the first) that includes the name of the article, the author (if available), the publication date of the material and the main idea (the thesis).
  - Other sentences that present in your own words the main points discussed in the article. **Remember!** The words are your own, but the ideas are not your own. They belong to the author of the article and should appear in your summary in the order in which they appeared in the original.
  - A final sentence that summarizes the conclusions made in the article.

4. Revising Your First Draft

- Revise your first draft.
- Check if you have summarized all the author's main points. If you didn't include all the main points, add the missing ones at this stage.
- If you included any minor points, eliminate them.
- Be sure you haven't included your own opinions in the summary.
- If your summary is too long, cut down words or phrases that are not absolutely necessary.

5. Writing a Second Draft

- If after stage 4 your summary looks messy and you cannot follow it clearly, write a second draft.

6. Editing

- Edit your summary.
- Make sure the spelling, grammar, punctuation and capitalization are correct.

Writing a One-Paragraph Summary
Illustration

Here is an illustration of the main steps in writing a summary:

? **8** *Read the article that follows and follow the steps in writing a summary.*

The Chinese New Year

The Chinese New Year, also called the Spring Festival is the most important festival for the Chinese people and a time for all the family to be together again. It is celebrated according to the Chinese calendar: it starts on the first day of the first lunar month and ends on the 15th, a day which is also called Lantern Festival. By the time it arrives, families have already spent days preparing the big event: cleaning and decorating the house, cooking festive foods, buying new clothes and gifts.

Foreigners wonder why the date for the Chinese New Year changes each year. This happens because the date is calculated according to the Chinese calendar, which is different from the Gregorian calendar, the most widely used calendar today. The Chinese calendar is considered to be the oldest calendar still in use. It is a combination of lunar and solar calendar, based on a number of complex astronomical calculations. The Chinese New year falls on the second new moon after the winter solstice (all months begin with a new moon).

How did the Chinese New Year come to be celebrated? Legend has it that people were once tormented by a beast called Nian (which means "year" in Chinese), a ferocious creature with a large mouth that could swallow several people at once. This beast would come the night before the New Year began to prey upon people. One day an old man who later proved to be a god came and rescued the people from the terrifying beast. He advised the villagers to put red decorations on their doors and windows to chase away Nian in case he returned. Therefore, each year people decorate their doors and windows with red paper and light firecrackers to scare away Nian. They also say the words "Guo Nian" which mean both "Survive the Nian" and "Celebrate the year." In fact, the Chinese New Year probably evolved from festivities celebrating the end of winter and rebirth associated with the coming of spring, just like the Roman festival Lupercalia. Nowadays, the Chinese New Year is mostly about family reunions, eating together, giving children red envelopes with money inside and wishing everyone good fortune in the year to come.

The Chinese New Year, also known as the Spring Festival is celebrated in many parts of South East Asia, such as China, Hong Kong, Taiwan, Malaysia, Vietnam, but not in Japan. The Japanese followed the lunar calendar until 1868, when they adopted the Gregorian calendar.

Prewriting
Writing the Main Idea
The Chinese New Year, also called the Spring Festival is celebrated for a whole month in various countries from SE Asia.

Note-Making
1. Chin. New Y - celebr. for a mnth.
2. Date changes. Based on Chin. calend. and falls 'on the second new moon after the winter solstice'.
3. Chin. New Y celebrates end of winter and coming of spring (cf. Roman Lupercalia). Now - a family celebr.
4. Spring Fest. celebrated in SE Asia, but not in Japan.

Writing a First Draft

?9 *Read this first draft and evaluate it against the checklist you devised earlier in this chapter. Write down the problems you have found in the space provided below:*

The article tries to answer some questions about the Chinese New Year: how long it lasts, when it is celebrated, how it started to be celebrated, where it is celebrated. Thus, the author shows that the date of the Chinese New Year, also called the Spring Festival, varies from one year to another because it is calculated according to the Chinese calendar, which is a complex solar/lunar calendar. There is a Chinese legend that explains how this festival came to be celebrated, but the author thinks that the real roots of the Chinese New Year are associated with the end of winter and the coming of spring. I agree with the author. Nowadays the Chinese New Year is a family celebration which lasts about a month: families get together, eat traditional food and children receive gifts of money in red envelopes. The Spring Festival is celebrated in China, Hong Kong, Malaysia, Taiwan, and Vietnam. It is not celebrated in Japan, because the Japanese follow the Gregorian calendar, not the Chinese calendar. (171 words)

Problems:

_____

_____

_____

_____

_____

_____

Writing a Second Draft. Revising and Editing.

? **10** *Read the second draft of the article. The content is correct, but there are eight mistakes. Find the mistakes and correct them.*

```
The article "The Chinese New Year" showing that the Chinese New
Year, also known as the Spring Festival is celebrated in various
Asian countries. The date changes every year because they are
calculated according to the Chinese calendar, a complex
solar/lunar calendar. The roots of the Chinese New Year are
associate with the rebirth and the come of spring. This festival
is celebrated in various Asia countries but not in Japan, because
Japan has adopted the Gregorian calendar. (80 words)
```

Now it's time for you to go through all these stages and write a one-paragraph summary.

? **11** *Complete the necessary steps to write a summary of the article below.*
1. *Read the article below once to determine its main idea.*

Human Matters?

Culture, a term coming from the Latin stem meaning "to cultivate", can be defined as beliefs, art, ways of life and institutions that are passed down from one generation to another. Culture refers to a society in which members share a common language, common rules of behavior and a basic social organization. Culture and society are somewhat interchangeable. But while some animals, such as wolves, bees or ants live in societies or groups, only humans can create and transmit culture.

Since the very beginnings of civilization, humans have exchanged culture in the form of ideas, people, natural resources and goods. Today, in our modern epoch of globalization, mass communication and consumerism, cultural and economic exchanges have witnessed dramatic soars, so that beside the national cultures, we can speak now of the creation of a global human culture.

Due to their capacity to adapt to new circumstances, humans can be considered one of the most successful species on the Earth. When there are changes in climate or other environmental changes, culture (in the broad sense) can help human societies survive and adapt. Thus, when the Earth warmed at the end of the last Ice Age, many animals that humans hunted for food disappeared, and a great part of land was covered with water. Yet people survived and adapted to the new circumstances, because they created new tools and learned how to use for food other species of plants and animals. Throughout the development of civilization, advances in medicine, technology, nutrition have led to the growth of the world population from about 6 million

in the Ice Age to about 6 billion today.

Unfortunately, the growth of culture and civilization has also led to many problems. Let us think about the last 200 years, the post Industrial Revolution period, marked by unprecedented developments in science and technology. As a direct result of extensive economic development, the past two centuries have witnessed an overuse of natural resources and energy and no concern for the environment. The direct consequences are what we see today: deforestation, endangered species, toxic waste, pollution, acid rain, global warming. If to these we add the consumption of essential natural resources, such as petroleum, natural gas, coal, timber, which outpaces nature's capacity to produce them, the picture becomes even gloomier. Luckily, it is still in our power to do something to save both our planet and ourselves from a possible disaster.

2. *Write the main idea of the article.*

_____
_____
_____

3. *Read the article again and take notes.*

_____
_____
_____
_____
_____

4. *Write a first draft of your summary. Include only the main points in the order in which they appear in the article.*

_____

_____

_____

_____

_____

_____

_____

_____

_____

_____

_____

5.*Swap your summary with a partner. Evaluate your partner's summary against the following checklist. Suggest improvements if necessary.*

Revising Checklist for Summaries

	Yes	No
1. Does the summary start with a sentence that gives the name of the article and the main idea?		
2. Does the summary include all the main points in the order in which they appear in the article?		
3. Did the author include minor points or personal opinions?		
4. Does the summary end with a sentence that sums up the author's conclusion?		
5. Is the summary expressed in your partner's own words?		
6. Is the summary • concise • clear • reader friendly		
7. Is the summary written in complete sentences?		
8. Are there any • spelling mistakes? • grammar mistakes? • punctuation mistakes?		

Note: If the summary you analyze is correct and effective, you should answer **"yes"** to questions **1, 2, 4, 5, 6, 7** and **"no"** to questions **3** and **8**.

6.*Read the comments made by your classmate. Write a second draft of your summary, taking into account his/her suggestions.*

7.*Revise and edit your second draft using the checklist above.*

TYPES OF ORAL PRESENTATIONS

Definition: What?

Making an oral presentation means preparing and delivering a speech on a specific topic in a clear, concise and logical form.

In real life people make various kinds of oral presentations. They can

- analyze problems
- offer recommendations and solutions
- present papers at conferences
- give progress reports
- give instructions on how to make or how to do something
- present project proposals
- describe the most important tourist sites in a certain area
- give an orientation tour
- try to persuade potential clients to buy a new product
- describe new developments in a certain field

Have you ever made an oral presentation?

?1 *Work in small groups. Make a list of the speaking situations, such as those above in which the members of your group made an oral presentation. Include situations in which you used your native language, as well as those in which you used English. Then sum up all the situations in the following table:*

Situation	Language used	
	Native language	**English**

Types of Delivery: How?

When preparing your presentation, you should consider both **what** to say (content) and **how** to say it (delivery). The way you prepare your presentation will depend to a great extent on the type of delivery you select.

There are four main styles or techniques of delivery:

1.Manuscript Presentations

A *manuscript presentation* is one that you write out completely and then read aloud to an audience. This type of presentation might be suitable only in very formal situations (e.g. academic or professional conferences) when the message to be delivered is very complex and technical. This is because manuscript presentations have serious disadvantages, as can be seen below.

Manuscript Presentations

Advantages	Disadvantages
• you do not need to rehearse giving your presentation	• it takes a long time to write your presentation in full sentences from beginning to end
• you can feel more secure	• you have little or no eye contact with the audience
	• difficult to adapt your presentation to suit the audiences' reactions
	• your voice does not sound natural and is often monotonous
	• difficult to keep the listeners' attention

Because of the serious disadvantages of reading a written report aloud, you are advised **not** to deliver manuscript presentations. Be cautious! Reading the text from the computer screen during a Power Point presentation session has the same disadvantages. Therefore, **do not** read the text word by word when giving a Power Point presentation!

2.Memorized Presentations

A *memorized* presentation is written out completely and then memorized word for word. Many students still prefer to use it. However, there are some serious disadvantages to this type, too.

? **2** *Work in groups. Have you ever delivered a memorized presentation? Try to make a list of the disadvantages of memorized presentations. Think about time, eye contact, voice, and other problems that may appear.*

Memorized Presentations

Advantages	Disadvantages

Due to their numerous disadvantages, memorized presentations should be avoided.

3.Impromptu Presentations

An *impromptu* presentation is one made on the spur of the moment, with little or no previous planning. Such presentations are usually demanded in certain specific work situations. For example, when you become a professional you may be asked to explain how your department is organized to a group of foreigners who have just arrived and wish to visit the company you work in. Even in such a situation, you should try to mentally organize your presentation and think about the first and last sentences.

Impromptu Presentations

Advantages	Disadvantages
• no specific preparation	• very difficult for a beginner in the field, because it requires good knowledge of the subject
• a lot of eye contact	• difficult to be well organized and efficient without any preparation
• you can get feedback from your audience and you can adjust your presentation as you speak	
• you can keep your audience interested by speaking in a natural manner	

Impromptu presentations are usually given by people who have a lot of experience in a certain field and who are also experienced in giving presentations. The more presentations you make, the easier it will be to give an impromptu presentation.

4.Extemporaneous Presentations

An *extemporaneous* presentation is carefully prepared and practiced in advance, without learning it word for word. As students, you should become used to giving this type of presentation, because it is the most common and the most effective of the four types. In the case of extemporaneous presentations, the ideas are thought in advance, but the speaker **does not** memorize the exact words.

When preparing such a presentation, you should
- determine subject, purpose and audience

- gather information
- plan your content and make an outline
- develop a strong introduction and conclusion
- practice your presentation

Extemporaneous Presentations

Advantages	Disadvantages
• you can have a lot of eye contact with the listeners	•it takes time to prepare and practice
• you can adapt your presentation to suit the audience's reactions	
• you can speak in a natural, conversational style	
• you can keep your audience's interest	

3 *Think about the oral presentations you have made so far. Which of the four types of delivery have you used?*

1. In the list below, tick (√) the delivery style(s) used in presentations made both in your mother tongue and in English.

Manuscript presentation   English ☐
                                             Native language ☐

Memorized presentation   English ☐
                                             Native language ☐

Impromptu presentation   English ☐
                                             Native language ☐

Extemporaneous presentation   English ☐
                                             Native language ☐

2. What were the problems you encountered when you prepared and delivered your presentation?

Making an Effective Presentation

How effective you presentation is depends on *delivery, content, organization,* and *language.*

Effective Delivery

Effective delivery refers to the way you use your eyes, body and voice to communicate what you have to say.

Eye contact is very important in keeping your audience's interest in the topic. It gives the listeners the feeling that you address them as individuals. It is also important for you as a speaker because you can see whether the listeners understand, are following and are interested in your message by watching their faces.

Some Tips
- Maintain good eye contact with all the audience.
- Move your eyes from person to person.
- Try not to look at one person all the time, because he/she may feel embarrassed.

Body Language and Posture

The way in which you use your posture, facial expressions and gestures conveys a significant message to your audience.

Some Tips
- Be poised and confident.
- Avoid rigidity.
- Avoid excessive informality – e.g. do **not** lean against a desk or a table.
- Do **not** put your hands in your pocket.
- Use a variety of gestures and facial expressions and synchronize them with the point you want to make. Avoid repeating the same gesture all the time.
- Avoid using too many gestures.
- Avoid distractors (do not play with a pencil; do not shift from one foot to another).

Voice is also very important in keeping your audience's interest and attention.

Some Tips
- Speak loud enough so that everyone can hear you.
- Vary the volume to draw the listeners' attention to the key points in your presentation.
- Speak at a proper rate (speed): neither too fast, nor too slow.
- Vary your rate of speech and use pauses to draw the listeners' attention to the key points in your presentation.
- Use a natural pitch of voice and vary it to prevent monotony.
- Speak in a natural, conversational manner.
- Pronounce your words clearly and correctly.
- Show enthusiasm for your subject.

? **4** *1. Work in groups. Use your personal experience and the tips above to make a list of **Do's** and **Don'ts** that should be taken into account when making an oral presentation:*

Do	Don't
keep eye contact with the audience	

2. Compare your lists in a class discussion. Agree upon a master list of guidelines.

? **5** *Individually prepare a 2 or 3 minutes presentation about something funny that happened to you.*

Work in groups. Take it in turns to make your presentations. During each presentation, the listeners will use the list with Do's and Don'ts to evaluate the speaker's delivery style. After each presentation, discuss the strengths and weaknesses, taking into account that the Do's count as strengths and the Don'ts count as weaknesses that need to be improved.

Preparing a Presentation
Before giving a presentation, you have to prepare it carefully. The next sections will help you prepare an efficient extemporaneous presentation.

The Elements of Good Oral Presentations: SPA
The elements of good oral presentations are: **subject, purpose,** and **audience (SPA)**.
When you start preparing your presentation
- select and limit your subject

- identify your purpose
- analyze your audience

Subject (What?)

When you make an oral presentation, one of the first questions you ask yourself is "What am I going to speak about?" In a professional environment, the subject and topic are usually determined in advance. At university level, the speaker has usually more freedom in choosing one's subject or topic.

In order to make a good oral presentation, select a topic
- that you understand and know well
- that interests you
- that is of potential interest to your listeners

Once you have chosen a general subject, it is helpful to narrow it down to a topic that can be covered in the time available. Otherwise, you either run out of time or present only a superficial view on the problem you want to discuss. Since usually your first choice is probably a large subject, a good idea is to narrow it down in several stages:

? **6** *Now it's your turn. Work in pairs and narrow down the following subjects:*

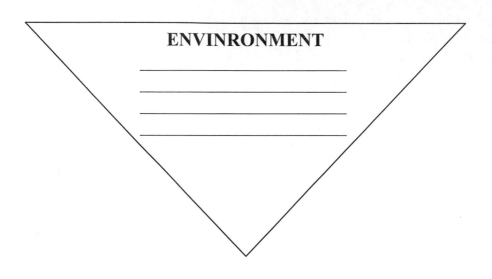

ENVINRONMENT

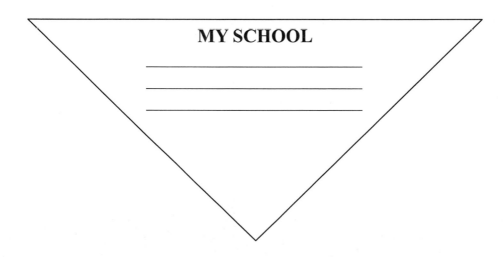

MY SCHOOL

Purpose

Other important questions you need to ask yourself are "Why am I speaking? What is my purpose?"

There are three main purposes for an oral presentation:

- **to inform**, i.e. to give your listeners new information that they want or they need to know;
- **to persuade**, i.e. to try to convince your listeners to do or make something (e.g. convince them to buy a certain product);
- **to entertain**, i.e. to provide an entertaining presentation for your listeners, without trying to convince them of something.

Remember that these purposes are **not** mutually exclusive and often appear in combinations: one and the same presentation can inform and persuade or persuade and entertain at the same time.

7 *Read the following selections of oral presentations. For each selection, write down the purpose: inform, persuade, entertain. If a selection has more than one purpose, specify all the purposes it may have. Be prepared to defend your answer.*

Selection 1: _____

Good morning everybody. I would like to start by asking you a very simple question: Have you ever eaten Italian pasta? I'm sure most of you have. You probably know that Italian pasta dishes are considered the best in the whole world. Today I'm going to show you that it is very simple to make "Mozzarella Pasta Penne", one of the famous Italian pasta dishes.

In order to prepare this dish, you need to cook the pasta in boiling water for about ten minutes…

Selection 2: _____

Good afternoon, ladies and gentlemen. Today I am going to speak to you about the history of computation. You might wonder why I have chosen this subject. The answer is quite straightforward: we have all studied calculus in school and we all know how to use a calculator, but how many of us know which the first computational aids were?

The first part of my presentation will try to answer this question; the second part will survey the present day development of computational devices, while the last part will offer you a glimpse of the future.

So, let us first go back in time to the early stages of human civilization. As early as 3000BC, numbers were in use in certain parts of the world. The first real computational aid, the abacus, was developed in China…

Selection 3: _____

Hello, everybody. Have you ever heard of *Cinderella*? *Cinderella* is a well-known fairy tale. It is a popular fairy tale about a beautiful, kind and unhappy girl whose mother had died. Her father then married a haughty woman who had two daughters of her own. The stepmother and her daughters forced Cinderella to work in the house, just like a servant, all day long. When evening came, she was allowed to sit by the fire, near the cinders. This is how the girl got her nickname, Cinderella…

Audience

One more important question you need to ask yourself is "Who are my listeners?" You should always gather as much information as possible about your audience's background and knowledge in order to be able to adapt your presentation to the needs and interests of your listeners. The specific audience you address to will affect your selection of the topic, your choice of words, the examples and details you present, and the amount of specialized information you include.

The worksheet below may help you build your audience profile:

Worksheet 1
Audience Profile
- Number of listeners
- Average age:
- Age range:
- Sex:
- Nationality:
- Ethnic groups:
- Level of education:
- Occupation:
- Specialization:
- Seating arrangements:
  in rows ☐   in a circle ☐   round a table ☐
- General level of English:
  advanced ☐   intermediate ☐   elementary ☐
- How much technical background do your listeners have?
  high ☐   medium ☐   low ☐
- How much do your listeners know about the subject of your presentation?
  very much ☐   something ☐   nothing ☐
- What do your listeners want or need to know?
- What do your listeners expect from you?

Some of these elements require further comments:

Level of English. Use words and structures that can be clearly understood by your audience.

Technical Knowledge. If your listeners are experts in the field, they will expect a lot of technical data. If they have little or no technical knowledge, use simple, nontechnical language.

Background Knowledge. Build your presentation on what your listeners already know. Do not repeat information they already know.

At this point it is important to consider other details of the speaking situation that may affect your presentation that can be seen in Worksheet 2.

Worksheet 2
Other Details of the Speaking Situation
- When is the presentation due? How much time do you have at your disposal?
- How many minutes are you going to speak?
- Where will the presentation take place?
- Are you going to stand, sit at a desk in front of the audience or sit with the listeners around a table?
- Is it going to be a formal, semiformal or informal situation?
- Will you use any facilities or visual aids?

8 *Work in groups. Use Worksheet 1 to analyze your class as an audience. Compare your results with other groups.*

9 *Work in small groups. Indicate whether the following topics are suitable (S) or unsuitable (U) to be given as oral presentations to your class. Consider whether each topic is:*
- *too limited*
- *too general*
- *too technical*
- *too well-known*

1. _____ Global Warming
2. _____ How to Improve Your Memory

3. _____ Ohm's Law
4. _____ New Year Celebrations in the World
5. _____ The University System in Different Countries
6. _____ Shakespeare's Tragedies
7. _____ The Organs of the Human Body
8. _____ Night Markets in Taiwan
9. _____ My Hometown
10. _____ Aspirin

?10 *1. Work in groups. Write down three topics that you think are suitable for a 7-10 minute presentation given to your class. Take into account the profile of your class as an audience.*

2. Swap your list with another group.

3. Look at the list written by the other group. Decide which of their topics are suitable for a 7-10 minute presentation. Consider whether the topic is
- *too limited*
- *too general*
- *too technical*
- *too well known*

If a topic is unsuitable, say why.

4. Take your list back. If your peers found that some of your topics are unsuitable, try to revise them to make them suitable.

MAKING ORAL PRESENTATIONS

Parts of an Oral Presentation
An oral presentation has three main parts: **introduction**, **body** and **conclusion.**

Functions of the Three Parts:
The Introduction
- attracts the listeners' interest
- focuses the listeners' attention on the topic (what the presentation is about)
- identifies the outline/steps of your presentation (how you are going to present your information)

The Body
- develops the main points of your presentation using a logical pattern of organization
- clarifies the main points
- supports your ideas with evidence

The Conclusion
- summarizes the main ideas of your presentation
- emphasizes your major conclusions
- can suggest a solution, a course of action or make a recommendation

The Introduction
The Introduction as an Incentive
As shown above, your introduction should catch your listeners' attention and should focus their attention on the topic. As a result, you should plan a **strong** introduction in order to make the audience want to hear your presentation. How can this be done? The best way to do this is to create common ground with your listeners, i.e., to relate your topic to their wants and needs.
When preparing your introduction, plan a base of shared experience and knowledge with your audience:

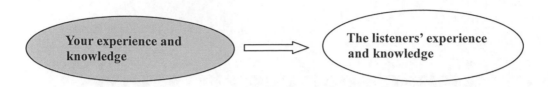

Then create common ground by linking separate experiences:

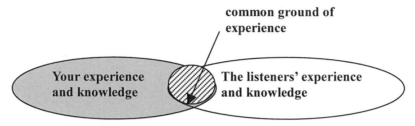

Techniques for Building a 'Strong' Introduction

In order to create common ground and get your listeners' attention, you can start with one or a combination of the following techniques:

- **an anecdote**

  An anecdote is an interesting, short and usually amusing personal account of an incident. In order to be effective, this story should be related to your topic. When the anecdote also gives the audience access to the background of your thinking, it creates a base of shared knowledge and experience which will permit the listeners to follow and rcspond to your ideas.

- **a quotation from an authority or expert**

  A quotation is a good way to introduce your topic. A well-chosen quotation can create immediate common ground with the audience because it gives both you and your listeners exactly the same words on which to reflect. You can also start your presentation by quoting a well-known proverb.

- **a question**

  Asking one or several questions is a good way to get your listeners' attention. They will try to give their own answer to your question(s) and will want to listen to your presentation to compare their answer to the one you give.

- **a surprising, unusual fact or happening**

  If you start with a surprising or unusual fact, your listeners are likely to show interest in your topic and see how it relates to the rest of your presentation.

- **impressive facts and statistics**
  By presenting interesting facts and statistics you can make your presentation more credible and interesting.

1 *Read the following introductions to oral presentations. In small groups, identify the technique(s) used in each one.*

1. All of us have some good friends – friends we can rely on, friends we confide in, friends we share our worries and joys with, friends who make our life easier and pleasant. But do you know who my best friend is? Do you know who our best friend is? He is the one who will never scold us if we forget about his birthday or if, as roommates, we forget to greet him in the morning and say "Good night" before going to bed. He will simply come and sit next to us, looking straight into our eyes to see what happened. He will never betray our friendship for money, position and will never be our rival in love. He will always be loyal and faithful. I'm sure you have guessed who I am talking about. Yes, you're right, I'm talking about dogs. They're our best friends. And if you are not already convinced about that, I'm pretty sure you'll become convinced about it before I finish my talk.

   Technique (s) _____

2. Good morning, everyone. I'm sure you all know the story of Cinderella, the sweet-tempered, hard-working girl who was obliged by her stepmother and her stepsisters to do all the housework and sleep in the cinders. Unfortunately, Cinderella story - and I'm not talking here about the movie – is real for many young children. Many children in underdeveloped countries live in poverty and some of them start work when they are extremely young. There is one big difference between such children and Cinderella. No prince has changed their life. At least not yet.

   Technique (s) _____

3. Due to our busy lives, it has become more and more difficult for us to find time to go from one department store to another in order to buy clothes, shoes, books, DVDs, electrical appliances or audio-video equipment. Starting with Jeff Bezos, the founder of *Amazon.com*, the first online bookstore, and indeed the first online store, many other entrepreneurs have used internet surfers as would be clients of their virtual stores. I'm pretty sure that most, if not all of you, have already shopped online. Shopping online seems much more convenient simply because you can do it without leaving your home, by pressing some keys on your computer. According to recent surveys, 38% of the

people surveyed prefer to shop on the web in order to avoid crowds. However, people have also become more aware of the possible dangers of online shopping. A recent survey shows that one out of five Brits avoid shopping online for fear of fraud.

Technique (s) _____

The Introduction as a Frame of Reference: Previewing a Presentation
Other functions of the introduction are to identify your topic and purpose and briefly introduce the main points of your presentation. This preview in terms of content and organization will offer your listeners a mental frame of reference, a "map" of your speech, and it will be easier for them to understand and remember what you present.
Let us go back to the first introduction in Activity 1 above and see how this may be done:

All of us have some good friends – friends we can rely on, friends we confide in, friends we share our worries and joys with, friends who make our life easier and pleasant. But do you know who my best friend is? Do you know who our best friend is? He is the one who will never scold us if we forget about his birthday or if, as roommates, we forget to greet him in the morning and say "Good night" before going to bed. He will simply come and sit next to us, looking straight into our eyes to see what happened. He will never betray our friendship for money, position and will never be our rival in love. He will always be loyal and faithful. I'm sure you have guessed who I am talking about. Yes, you're right, I'm talking about dogs. They're our best friends. And if you are not already convinced about that, I'm pretty sure you'll become convinced about that before I finish my talk.

So, my speech is about dogs, man's best friends. First, I'm going to tell you how this happened, I mean, how dogs became man's best friend. Next, I will present some interesting and maybe less known dog breeds. Finally, I will tell you some amazing real stories in which dogs were the main protagonists.

Language Used in Introductions
Introducing the Topic

I'm going to I will I'd like to	deal with present speak about talk about
This presentation will	analyze be about compare deal with discuss examine explain focus on suggest/propose

Previewing

This presentation	has falls into is divided into	_____ parts
There are	_____ parts	to this presentation

First, Next, Then, Third(ly), Finally,	I'd like to I'm going to I will	review… speak about… deal with…

2 *1. Work in groups of 3-4. Choose one of the following subjects*:

1. My Hometown
2. My University
3. Traditional Celebrations
4. Tourist Spots in _____ (write the name of a country)
5. How to Prepare _____ (write the name of your favorite dish)
6. The Best Way to Learn English
7. How to Find a Job
8. Advantages and Disadvantages of Using Computers
9. How to Avoid Being a Couch Potato
10. Comparing Printed Books and e-Books

2. Work individually to prepare an effective one-to two minute introduction to a presentation on the subject chosen. Specify
- *subject*
- *purpose*
- *audience*

*3. Choose a specific technique to build a strong introduction. Each student in the group should choose a **different** technique. Introduce your topic and make a preview of your presentation. Select suitable language from the tables above.*

4. When everyone has finished, take turns presenting your introductions to the group. Discuss the strengths and weaknesses of each introduction.
Use the following checklist:

Revising Checklist for Introductions to Oral Presentations

	Yes	No
1. Does the introduction create interest in the topic?		
2. Does the introduction specify the topic?		
3. Does the introduction preview the topic?		
4. Does the speaker use specific language to introduce and preview the topic?		

The Body

Determining Your Central Idea

The body of your presentation is the largest part in which you state, discuss, develop, explain, and clarify your ideas. In order to do this, you need to develop a clear central idea, which is in fact the main point of your presentation. Always ask yourself: "What do I want to do?"

For example, if your general subject is pollution, your central idea might be

- to analyze some causes and/or some effects of pollution
- to explain and discuss various types of pollution
- to give some solutions on how to cut down pollution
- to compare pollution factors in two different countries
- to discuss the advantages of pollution free vehicles

? **3** *Work in groups. Determine at least two different interesting topics, each with a clear central idea, based on* **one** *the following subjects:*

1. Traditional celebrations
2. Robots
3. Computers
4. Cities
5. Movies
6. Food
7. Television
8. Universities
9. Traveling
10. Money

Organizing the Main Points

The body of your presentation includes the main points and details, examples, facts or figures that develop the central idea. In order to make your presentation clear to follow and easy to understand, you should do two important things:

- Arrange your ideas in a logical order or *pattern of organization* that is suitable to your topic.
- Use *transitions*.

Patterns of Organization

A. Time (Chronological Order)
This pattern of organization arranges events as they occur in time. The key question is *when?* Use this pattern if you **tell a story**, **give instructions**, **explain steps of a procedure**, or **discuss how something developed in time**.

1. Central idea: telling a story

   or

   giving instructions

   Body:
   I. First
   II. Next
   III. Then
   IV. Finally

2. Central idea: explaining steps of a procedure
   Body:
   I. First step
   II. Second step
   III. Third step
   IV. Fourth step

3. Central idea: discussing how something developed in time
   Body:
   I. Past
   II. Present
   III. Future

Transitions That Signal Chronological Order

first	before	when
second	earlier	after that
third	during	later
fourth	at that time	as

next	while	as soon as
then	meanwhile	at last
finally	by the time	in the present/ past/ future

B. Spatial Order

This patterns arranges objects according to spatial location or direction, such as

- from far to near
- from east to west
- from north to south
- from inside to outside
- from top to bottom
- from left to right

The key question is *where?* Use this pattern when you **describe an object**, **a building**, **a place**.

1. Central idea: describing an object
   Body:
   I. Top
   II. Middle
   III. Bottom

2. Central idea: describing a building
   Body:
   I. Location
   II. General description (outside)
   III. First floor
   IV. Second floor
   V. Third floor
   VI. Top floor

3. Central idea: describing a place
   Body:
   I. Geographical position
   II. Central part
   III. Eastern side
   IV. Western side
   V. Southern side
   VI. Northern side

Transitions That Signal Spatial Order

above	beside	to the left
below	between	to the right
at the center	near	north/south/east/west
in front of	next to	top/bottom
behind	across	outside/inside

C. Topical Order (Order of Importance)

This pattern divides a larger topic into several subtopics. You can order your ideas in various ways:

- from the least important to the most important
- from the most important to the least important
- from general to specific
- from specific to general
- from the known to the unknown
- from simple to complex

The key question is *what?* Use this organization pattern if you want to **classify into categories, analyze causes and/or effects of a situation, describe a problem and give solutions, compare and contrast two objects/situations, give arguments for/against, show advantages and disadvantages**.

This pattern includes several subdivisions:

1. Central idea: classifying
   Body:
   I. First category
   II. Second category
   III. Third category
   IV. Fourth category

Transitions That Signal Classifications

There are three/four/five kinds/types/classes/categories/groups of…	_ can be classified/divided/grouped into several types/classes/categories	The first/second/third type/class/category/group is…
There are several/ many kinds/types/classes/categories/groups of…	_ consists of/includes three/four/several types/classes/categories	First,…/Second,…/Third,…/Finally,…
_ can be classified/ divided into three/four kinds/types/classes/groups	There are three/four/ several types/classes/ categories of…	One class/category…; Another class/category…

2. Central idea: explaining the main causes of a situation
   Body:
   I. Explanation of the situation (and possible effects)
   II. First cause
   III. Second cause
   IV. Third cause
   V. Fourth cause

3. Central idea: explaining the effects of a situation
   Body
   I. Explanation of the situation (and possible causes)
   II. First effect
   III. Second effect
   IV. Third effect

Transitions That Signal Cause and Effect Relationships

because	for this reason	since
because of	that is why	so
as a result of	due to	therefore
consequently	owing to	thus

4. Central idea: describing a problem and giving solutions
   Body:
   I. Defining the problem (causes and effects)
   II. Solution 1
   III. Solution 2
   IV. Solution 3
   V. Solution 4

5. Central idea: comparing and contrasting
   To compare means to discuss similarities between people, places, objects, events, ideas.
   To contrast means to discuss differences. There are two main patterns that can be used
   when you compare and contrast: the **block method** and the **point-by point method**.
   If you use the block method, you first describe all the similarities and then all the
   differences. If you use the point-by point method, you identify several points of
   comparison (criteria) as the basis of your organization. Then you discuss the two things
   point by point.

   Body: comparing and contrasting (block pattern)
   I. Similarities
   II. Differences

Body: comparing and contrasting (the point-by-point pattern)
I. Comparing and contrasting two things according to the first point
   (criterion)
II. Comparing and contrasting two things according to the second point
    (criterion)
III. Comparing and contrasting two things according to the third point
     (criterion)
IV. Comparing and contrasting two things according to the fourth point

Transitions That Signal Comparison

similarly	as...as	in the same way
similar to	both...and	also
like	the same (as)	too
likewise	just as...	A..., and so does B

Transitions That Signal Contrast

while	however	in contrast (to)
whereas	unlike	contrary to
although	but	in spite of
even though	on the other hand	different from

6. Central idea: giving reasons for/against
   Body:
   I. Reasons against
   II. Reasons for

   or

   I. Reasons for
   II. Reasons against

Transitions That Express Reasons

There are three/four arguments for/against...	For one thing.../For another...
The main reason/argument for/against is...	First, due to...; Second...
One reason is.../Another reason is...	Because, first...; and second...

7. Central idea: showing advantages and disadvantages
   This can be seen as a subcategory of the previous pattern.
   Body:
   I. Disadvantages
   II. Advantages

   or

   I. Advantages
   II. Disadvantages

Transitions That Signal Advantages/Disadvantages

There are three/four (dis)advantages…	The first/second (dis)advantage is that…
The most important (dis)advantage is that…	The drawback is that…

Other Transitions

Transitions are the words or phrases that connect and show the relationship of your ideas. By linking your ideas, transitions help your listeners follow your progress from one part of the presentation to another.

There are other useful transitions you might use in the body of your presentation:

Introducing the First Point

Let us start with…	To begin with,…
The first thing I'd like to do is to…	The first thing/point/advantage/reason/ step/cause/effect I would like to speak about/deal with is…

Moving to Other Points

The second/third/fourth main point/ advantage/reason/step/cause/effect is	Now, let's turn to…
Let's now move on to…	I now want to go on to…

? **4** *Here are some more transitions used to* **add ideas**, **exemplify** *and* **explain/ reformulate**. *Work in pairs. Insert the words and phrases below under the proper heading:*

for example in other words in addition furthermore namely	moreover that is to illustrate to put it differently what's more	to put it another way as an illustration also for instance such as

Additional Ideas	**Giving Examples**	**Explaining/Reformulating**

? **5** *Work in small groups. Match each of the following topics (1-10) with the most suitable pattern of organization (a-g). You might need to use some patterns more than once.*

a. chronological
b. spatial
c. classification
d. cause and effect
e. problem solution
f. comparison and contrast
g. reasons for and against

_____ 1. Types of books
_____ 2. How an eye and a camera are similar
_____ 3. Advantages and disadvantages of nuclear power stations
_____ 4. Effects of pollution on the environment
_____ 5. Taipei 101
_____ 6. How to start a business
_____ 7. Energy sources in the twenty-first century
_____ 8. Describing my hometown
_____ 9. Watching television: pros and cons
_____10. How to prepare for an exam

? **6** *As a class, choose **one** of the following general subject areas:*

• The Environment
• Travel
• Students
• Food
• Celebrations

1. Work individually to develop the subject you chose into two different topics, each with a clear central idea and a specific pattern of organization. Complete the following:
Subject:_____

Topic 1: central idea _____
Pattern of organization _____
Topic 2: central idea _____
Pattern of organization _____

2. *Now work in small groups. Combine your ideas to make a list of at least **five** different topics, each with a clear central idea. Write them on a sheet of paper (the List of Topics) Include topics that require **different** patterns of organization. Write the pattern of organization corresponding to each topic on **another** list (the Answer Sheet).*

3. *Exchange your Lists of Topics with another group. Keep your Answer Sheets. Try to decide which pattern of organization best suits each of the topics on the other group's list. Write your ideas at the bottom of the other group's List of Topics.*

4. *Compare your ideas with the other group and reach agreement on the best pattern of organization.*

The Conclusion

The conclusion is the final point of contact between you and the audience. Just like the introduction it is a very important part of your presentation because the listeners remember best what they hear first and last. Therefore, you need to bring all the threads together, while also leaving a strong impression on the audience.

Thus, the conclusion should have a double purpose:

- summarizing the main ideas of your presentation
- leaving a strong impression on the audience

There is no right way to conclude a presentation. There are, however, some techniques you can use:

Techniques used for concluding an oral presentation

- **Summarize or review your main points**

    At the end of your presentation, you need to restate your main points. Try **not** to repeat the same words. Find out a new way to express your ideas.

- **Suggest a solution/Make a recommendation**

    Depending on your subject, you can end your presentation by suggesting a solution or making a recommendation.

- **Give the audience food for thought**

    You can
    a.ask your listeners a puzzling or provocative question
    b.ask your listeners to speculate on the future
    c.ask your listeners to reflect on the past

- **Ask the listeners to take a stand**

    You can ask your listeners to take a stand and **do** something in order to solve a problem. This kind of conclusion is appropriate if, for example, your presentation was about environmental protection.

Language Used for Concluding an Oral Presentation
Summarizing/Concluding

to summarize	to conclude
to sum up	in short
on the whole	in the end
in brief	in conclusion

Closing One's Presentation

Before closing, I would like to…	In closing,…
I would like to close by saying that…	Let me close by…

7 *Read the following conclusions to oral presentations. In small groups, identify the technique(s) used in each one.*

1. In conclusion, I think that whenever a decision about robots is being made, those who take such decisions should consider the arguments for and the arguments against. But the real problem is another one: Can robots totally replace humans in the future? Let us all try to answer this question.

   Technique(s) _____

2. To conclude, I think that we all need to be aware that the environment should be protected. Planet Earth is our legacy for the next generations. What can we do? There are many things we can do and, although they may seem unimportant, by doing them we can help our environment become healthier and cleaner for the generations to come. Here are some of the things you can do:
   - Walk or use bicycles instead of scooters, motorcycles or cars.
   - Recycle.
   - Do not throw litter in the street or in forests after picnicking.
   - Switch off the lights and your electrical appliances when you don't use them.
   - Consume less power and water.
   - Buy green, buy local, buy used and buy less.

   Technique(s) _____

3. To sum up, we can say that robots are a blessing, because of the advantages of using them. But they can also be seen as a curse, because I think that in time they will totally replace humans in any activity.

   Technique(s) _____

?8 *1. Work in groups of 3-4. Choose one of the following subjects:*

1. My Hometown
2. My University
3. Traditional Celebrations
4. Tourist Spots in _____ (write the name of a country)
5. How to Prepare _____ (write the name of your favorite dish)
6. The Best Way to Learn English
7. How to Find a Job
8. Advantages and Disadvantages of Using Computers
9. How to Avoid Being a Couch Potato
10. Comparing Printed Books and e-Books

2. Work individually to prepare an effective one-to two minute conclusion to a presentation on the subject chosen.

*3. Choose a specific technique to build a strong conclusion. Each student in the group should choose a **different** technique. Select suitable language from the tables above.*

4. When everyone has finished, take turns presenting your conclusions to the group. Discuss the strengths and weaknesses of each conclusion.
   Use the following checklist:

Revising Checklist for Conclusions to Oral Presentations

	Yes	No
1. Does the conclusion summarize the main points of the presentation?		
2. Is the conclusion interesting?		
3. Does the speaker use specific language to conclude and close the presentation?		

Writing an Outline

When you prepare your presentation you should write an outline to organize the information you want to include. Here is a model of such an outline:

Name:
Topic: Robots: a blessing or a curse?
Pattern of organization: reasons for and against

Introduction

I. Background
  A. The progress of technology has led to the development of complex machines, called robots, designed to help and even replace humans.
  B. The use of robots in industry is a blessing for some people and a curse for others.

II. History
  A. The word "robot" comes from the Czech word robota meaning "serf worker" or "slave".
  B. The word was first used in the play R.U.R. (Rossum's Universal Robots), written by the Czech writer Karel Čapek and performed in 1920.

III. Definition
  A robot is a re-programmable machine that can perform different tasks.

Body

I. Arguments for
  A. Accuracy (provide examples, facts and figures)
  B. Higher productivity (provide facts and figures)
  C. Robots can work in dangerous places (provide examples)
  D. Robots can do the hard work for us (provide examples)

II. Arguments against
  A.Robots are expensive (provide figures)
  B. Robots can have malfunctions and this can lead to disasters
  C. Unemployment (provide examples)

Conclusion

I. Sum up arguments and counterarguments
II. State the speaker's point of view
III. End up with a question meant to involve the listeners

Now it's your turn to write such an outline

 9 *1. Work individually. Select one the following general subjects below.*

1. Traditional celebrations
2. Education
3. Computers
4. Cities

5. Movies
6. Food
7. Television
8. Universities
9. Traveling
10.Money

2. Limit your subject to an interesting topic with a clear central idea and select a suitable pattern of organization. Then complete the outline form below:

Name:
Topic:
Central idea:
Pattern of organization:

Introduction

   I. _____

      A. _____

      B. _____

   II. _____

      A. _____

      B. _____

   III. _____

      A. _____

      B. _____

Body

   I. _____

      A. _____

      B. _____

   II. _____

      A. _____

      B. _____

   III. _____

      A. _____

      B. _____

  IV. _____

      A. _____

      B. _____

Conclusion

  I. _____

  II. _____

3. Prepare a five minute presentation. Look at the checklist below to see how you will be evaluated.

4. Deliver your presentations in turns in small groups. The other students who are listening should complete the checklist below.

Oral Presentations Checklist

Speaker:

Topic:

	Yes	No	Comments
Delivery			
Does the speaker use a natural, conversational style (not read or memorized word for word)?			
Is the volume loud enough?			
Is the rate of speech appropriate (neither too fast, nor too slow)?			
Does the speaker have eye contact with the audience?			
Is the speaker's body posture appropriate?			
Content and organization			
Is the topic suitable for the audience?			
Is the topic suitable for the time available (neither too broad nor too narrow)?			

Is there a clear central idea?			
Does the presentation fall into three parts (introduction, body, conclusion)?			
Does the introduction specify the topic?			
Does the introduction preview the topic?			
Does the introduction create interest in the topic?			
Are the main points clearly stated?			
Are the main points supported by relevant details, facts, examples?			
Does the conclusion summarize the main points of the presentation?			
Does the speaker use suitable transitions in all the introduction, body and conclusion?			
Accuracy and fluency			
Does the speaker use correct grammar structures?			
Does the speaker use vocabulary appropriate for the audience?			
Does the speaker pronounce all the words correctly?			
Does the speaker express his/her ideas fluently?			
Visual aids			
Does the speaker use any visual aids?			
Are the visual aids easy to see and clear?			
Are the visual aids helpful in clarifying the topic?			

WRITING RESEARCH PAPERS

As a student, you will be frequently asked to write reports and term papers for various subjects, so it is a good thing to know the basics while still a freshman.

Structure of a Research Paper

Preliminaries	1. Title
	2. Acknowledgements
	3. Contents / List of contents
	4. List of figures/tables/diagrams/photographs
Introduction	5. Introducing field and topic
	6. Summarizing previous research
	7. Finding a niche
	8. Introducing present research
Main body	9. Review of literature
	10. Design of the investigation
	11. Methods and procedures/ Measurement techniques/ Instruments used
	12. Results
	13. Discussion of results
Conclusion	14. Summary of conclusions
Extras	15. Bibliography
	16. Appendices

?1 *Check your understanding of the following words, by matching them with their definition or synonyms:*

1. ___ acknowledgements	a. area, subject, domain
2. ___ field (in research)	b. hollow place; activity, position or job which is suitable for someone
3. ___ niche	c. additional information at the end of a book or a paper
4. ___ appendix	d. author's thanks addressed to those who have helped
5. ___ hypothesis (sg.) hypotheses (pl.)	e. a tentative explanation for a phenomenon, used as a basis for further investigation in a study

There may be slight variations to the framework above. For example, *Acknowledgements* can appear before or after the *List of contents*. If *Summarizing previous research* in the *Introduction* is rather comprehensive, then the *Review of literature* section need not appear in the main body of the report. If it is brief, it will be followed by a special section in the main body. Other items, such as *Dedication, List of abbreviations* can be included in the **Preliminaries.**

? 2 *Below you can find descriptions (a-p) of each section (1-16) in a research report. Decide which description goes with which section. Write the corresponding letter in each box:*

1	2	3	4	5	6	7	8	9	10	11	12	13	14	15	16

a) The presentation of data usually in the form of tables or graphs.
b) Additional data and illustrative material placed at the end of the paper (outside the body of the text).
c) Detailed description and discussion of testing devices or instruments used.
d) A presentation of the field and topic under study.
e) A statement of the hypothesis and the theoretical structure in which it will be tested and examined.
f) The sections and subsections with a corresponding page number.
g) A brief account of the main findings, and the possible implications or effects.
h) The first element that appears and describes the paper in the fewest words possible.
i) Author's thanks addressed to those who have helped.
j) A critical account of previous research in that specific field.
k) The sequence of tables, charts or diagrams that appear in the text with the corresponding page number.
l) A survey of relevant reading of the literature.

m) The listing in alphabetical order of all the sources quoted in the text.

n) Establishing a niche in current knowledge or that topic which might be occupied by your piece of research.

o) A brief discussion of your research and the reasons for undertaking it.

p) The interpretation of expected and unexpected results and of their relationship to the research problem and hypotheses.

This general framework will have variations as far as the **introduction**, **body** and **conclusion** are concerned, depending on your field of investigation and your purpose.

Framework for Literature Papers
Introduction

- Identify the author and literary work you are going to analyze
- Provide some background information about the writer and the literary work you are going to speak about
- Summarize previous research
- Introduce present research; present your thesis

Body

- Review of literature (accompanied by relevant quotations and paraphrases from significant works)
- Literary analysis (depending on your topic you can analyze plot, theme, character development, narrative technique, imagery, language, etc)

Conclusion

- Bring threads together: highlight the writer's contributions and importance in clear relationship to the topic of your study

Framework for Comparative Study
Introduction

Provide background information about topic

Identify A and B (the two things to be compared and contrasted)

Summarize previous research

Introduce present research; present your thesis

Body

You can choose from 3 possible methods of organization.

1.
- Analyze A
- Analyze B
- Compare and contrast A and B

2.
- Compare A and B (show what is similar)
- Contrast A and B (show what is different)

3.
- Issue 1 - Compare and contrast A and B
- Issue 2 - Compare and contrast A and B
- Issue 3 - Compare and contrast A and B

Conclusion
- Bring threads together: summarize similarities and differences
- Draw a conclusion

The Research Process
Writing a research paper covers several stages:
- Finding a topic and formulating a title
- Generating ideas
- Doing preliminary research – find relevant sources
- Devising a working thesis
- Gathering information
- Creating a working bibliography
- Creating effective notes
- Writing an outline
- Writing first draft
- Revising and editing
- Preparing manuscript in MLA or APA style

These stages are not linear: writing is a *recursive* process, characterized by many movements back and forth.

Preparing a Research Paper
Just as in the case of oral presentations, you have to think carefully and plan your work with great attention before writing a research paper. Before choosing a topic and title, you need to try to answer the following questions:
- What is the submission date?
- How many words or pages do you have to write?
- What style or format should you use?
- Are there any intermediate deadlines, e.g. literature review, presenting a proposal, writing the first draft?
- What tutorial support is available?

Finding a Topic

One of the crucial things to do when you need to write a research paper is to choose a topic. Normally there are three possible situations:

1. **Assigned topic**. The topic is given by your teacher. In such a situation, you do not have to bother about finding a topic because it is a *given* and you can go directly to the next stage.

2. **Course related topic.** In such a case you are asked to investigate a subject that is related to the material covered in a specific course. You can either be given a list of possible topics to choose from or you devise your own topic on condition it is related to that specific course.

? 3 *Work with a partner. Identify 2 possible topics of investigation for "Introduction to Western Literature" and 2 for "Introduction to Linguistics."*

3. **Unrestricted topic**. You are completely free to choose your own topic. This seems to be an easy thing to do, yet at first it might be a difficult experience, something like having a microphone thrust in your face and being told to say anything you want. It is at this precise moment that you feel your head is empty and you have nothing to say. However, do not worry, this happens to many people. It doesn't matter so much where you start from as long as you **do** start.

How can you choose a topic?

- You can start with yourself. What do you like doing? What are your hobbies and interests? What puzzles you?

- You can also think of your everyday activities: you eat, go to school, wear clothes, go shopping, watch TV, play the computer, listen to music, practice sports, read books. Any of these may represent a subject for your paper.

- You can also think of your surroundings: your street, your city, county, country, natural scenery, historic landmarks, important buildings, etc.

- You can also choose a topic related to the books you have read, recent newspaper articles, or important issues in our society.

? 4 *Write down two problems you might want to investigate related to the categories mentioned above.*

Here are some do's and don'ts for selecting a topic:

Choose a problem	Don't choose a problem
• that interests you	• you know nothing about
• that is of potential interest to other people	• to which the answer is just "yes" or "no", without explaining the reasons. Remember that in research we need to know why things are as they are and how they work.
• that you can find information about	• that involves merely a comparison of two sets of data without revealing something new. Research means looking beyond results to find something new.

Focus Your Topic

It is important to focus your topic so that you can adequately cover it in your paper. The technique is similar to that presented in the chapter on "Oral presentations." Here are some examples:

English literature	Superstitions	Culture
English drama	Chinese superstitions	Aboriginal culture
William Shakespeare	Chinese superstitions about New Year	Amis culture
Animal imagery in Macbeth	Superstitions about New Year among college students in Taiwan	Harvest ceremony in Amis culture

A Word of Caution

Some kinds of topics are difficult, if not impossible to complete in a satisfactory manner in your research paper. They include the following categories:

- **Broad Topics**

  If your topic is too broad, you will find that you need a lot of time to read all available sources. You may also need to write several hundreds or even thousands of pages to cover all you have to say about the respective subject. Examples of such broad subjects are those in the upper boxes above. Other such examples include "American fiction", "Varieties of English" or "First person narrators in 19th century fiction". Such subjects need to be narrowed down as shown above before starting to write your paper.

- **Narrow Topics/Limited Sources**
  If your topic is too narrow or limited, you will not find enough sources of information (books, articles). Normally you need to read and use at least 10 sources (periodicals, books, electronic sources, etc). If you choose a 'hot' topic that is covered only in recent newspapers, it will not be enough to back up your ideas. For example if you choose to write about "Parks in Chisan" it will be hard to find enough sources.

- **Technical Topics**
  As an undergraduate student try to avoid topics that require specialized knowledge you may not yet possess. For example do not choose a topic such as "Conversational implicature in classroom discourse" if you are not familiar with the concepts and terminology of pragmatics and discourse analysis.

- **Subjective Topics**
  As shown above, the subject you choose for your paper should interest you. This does not mean that the research paper you write will be about your own opinion on a certain issue. Stating personal opinion is not research. Your ideas should be supported by other people's views, by reasons, explanations, facts and figures.

- **Clichéd Topics**
  Avoid topics that are too obvious, too well known or that have been discussed to death. Example of such topics might include "Analyzing *Hamlet*", "Egyptian pyramids" or "Flying saucers". Such topics are predictable and will probably bring nothing new. Choose a topic that is interesting and original both for you and your reader.

5 *Work in small groups. Consider the following topics. Do you think they are suitable for investigation in a research paper? Write **Yes**, **No** or **Possibly** next to each problem. Prepare to defend your options.*

1. _____A study that compares the results in the College Entrance Examination in Taiwan in the past five years.
2. _____Female characters in Shakespeare's comedies.
3. _____A comparison of internet shopping habits in Taiwan and Thailand.
4. _____The influence of various parenting styles on the development of social skills in teenagers.
5. _____A reexamination of the "critical period hypothesis".
6. _____Various roles assumed by Dr. Watson in Conan Doyle's stories.
7. _____The impact of globalization on the job market in South East Asia.

8. _____Why do Chinese students find it difficult to communicate in English?
9. _____Chinese and Western superstitions: a comparison.
10. _____Cross cultural differences: focus on Westerners living in Taiwan.

Discovering and Generating Ideas for Your Research Report
There are three complementary techniques for doing this:
- talk to one or two authorities on the subject (your professor, maybe also someone else);
- use a research diary or log to jot down ideas and questions that may occur to you or reactions to the materials you are reading.
- use some of the techniques for generating ideas

Techniques for Generating Ideas
There are many techniques for generating ideas. The main ones are presented below

Brainstorming
The object of this technique for generating ideas is to write quickly and, once finished, to return to your work with a critical eye. In order to brainstorm ideas:
- Place your topic at the top of a page;
Set a time limit (5 or 10 minutes);
- List items related to the topic as quickly as you can.
At this stage, all items are legitimate for your list, because a good idea can emerge out of what seems to be a bad idea.

Illustration: Robotic Systems

- can work in dangerous environments	- space
- automaton	- underwater
- industrial robot	- have to be programmed
- can have malfunctions	- high costs
- at home (domestic robots)	- speed
- high accuracy	- productivity
- cyborg	- android
- unemployment	- industry

After ideas have been generated and written they are *organized*, i.e. grouped into related items. Those that do not fit into a grouping are set aside. Groupings with the greatest number of items indicate areas that may prove to be particularly fertile in developing your piece of writing.

Types of robots:	Uses:	Advantages:	Disadvantages:
automaton	industry	high accuracy	have to be programmed
industrial robot	at home	speed	consequence - unemployment
android	space	productivity	high costs
cyborg	underwater	can work in dangerous environments	can have malfunctions

6 *In the space provided below, brainstorm ideas on the topic* **Chinese and Western Superstitions**.

_____

_____

_____

_____

_____

7 *Now, group similar ideas together and give each group a heading. Eliminate ideas that do not fit in.*

_____

_____

_____

_____

_____

_____

Clustering (Mapping) Using the Journalist's Questions

This is a technique used both for generating and organizing ideas. It is particularity useful if you enjoy thinking visually. Here are the steps you need to take if you apply this technique:

- Write the topic in the middle of the page;
- Circle the topic;
- Draw several short spokes from the circle (3-6);

Illustration:
Clustering

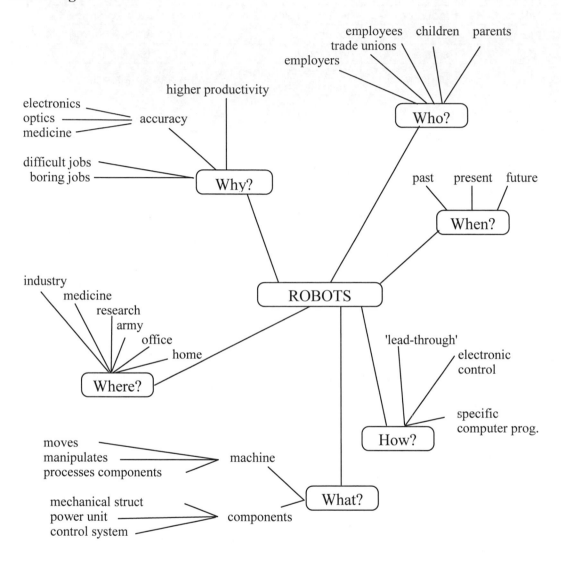

- At the end of each spoke place one of the journalist's questions (*who, what, where, when, why, how*);
- Make a major branch off the spoke for each answer to a question. In answering these questions you can in fact *define, compare, contrast,* or *investigate cause and effect*;
- Take each answer individually and ask one of the six journalist's questions again.

When you have completed this activity, you will have a page that places ideas in relation to each other. Moreover, the map distinguishes between major points (main branches) and supporting information (secondary branches).

? **8** *In the space below, practice the clustering technique for the topic* **Chinese and Western Superstitions**.

Freewriting

Freewriting is a warm-up technique, meant to help you overcome the *writer's block*. To practice this technique, take a watch or a clock and follow these steps:

- Look at the topic you need to write about;
- Write down a sentence stating you point of view at the top of a blank sheet of paper;
- Starting from the topic question, write for five minutes **without interruption. Do not stop writing**. If you are at a loss, you can just write "I cannot think of anything...I cannot think of anything..." or "My mind is blank...My mind is blank..."
- After **exactly** five minutes, stop writing;
- Read over what you have written;
- Summarize the main idea in a single sentence;
- Write this new sentence at the top of a second sheet of paper;
- Using this new sentence as a starting point, write again for five minutes. **Do not stop writing**!
- Read again what you have written;
- Summarize the main idea in a single sentence;
- Write this idea at the top of a third sheet of paper;

- Repeat the stages until you feel you have overcome the *writer's block*.
  At the end of this process you will realize that:
  a) You have produced a great number of words in English.
  b) You have discovered what you wanted to say on that particular subject.

Focused Freewriting

Focused freewriting is a technique that offers you the benefits of freewriting while keeping your attention focused on the topic:

- Start with a definite topic;
- Write for five minutes;
- Read over what you have written;
- Circle any words, phrases and sentences that look potentially useful;
- Group these items either at the bottom of the page or on a separate sheet of paper.

Following is a portion of a student's focused freewriting around the topic *Robots - A Mixed Blessing*.

Illustration:
Focused Freewriting

(...) On the one hand robots are useful in industry because they (work full time), they have a very big (accuracy) and they can work (in dangerous places) ; they can (also increase production) and they use an advanced technology, giving products of a (better quality).

On the other hand, they (can have malfunctions) and if a robot stops, the whole production line can be stopped. After a period of time, robots (must be replaced) because they (do not last long).

This piece of freewriting can be further organized into the following notes meant to be expanded.

Robots

Advantages	Disadvantages
- work full time	- can have malfunctions
- work in dangerous places	- if a robot stops → the whole production line can stop
- lead to increased prod.	
- make better-quality prod.	- do not last long - have to be replaced

The 'Many Parts' Technique

This method for generating ideas consists in listing its parts and then making notes about the **uses** or **consequences** of some or of all the parts enlisted.

Illustration

e.g. What are the 'parts' (i.e. types) of robots?

1. automata
2. robotic systems
3. androids
4. cyborgs

One Part Explored

What are the uses of robotic systems?
- industry
  - production lines (welding)
  - materials handling
  - assembly (electronic parts)
  - inspection
- military
  - automatic pilot
  - defuse bombs
  - control modern weapons
- ocean
  - explorer
- space
  - lift satellites out of spacecrafts
  - put satellites into orbit
  - stationary observer
    - collect samples
    - take photos
- office
  - clerk
  - mail handler
- home
  - companion
  - housekeeper
    - cleaning
    - cooking

What are the consequences of using robotic systems?
- higher productivity
- accuracy
- hard and dangerous work will not be performed by humans
- employees will be mostly knowledge workers
- possibility of totally replacing humans in industry
- unemployment
- disasters (if one part of the system breaks, everything may fall apart)

Devising a Working Thesis

Once you have ideas about your topic you are ready for the next step–finding a **thesis**. A **thesis** is a single-sentence statement that summarizes your controlling idea, the position you support or the point you want to make. At this early stage you are not supposed to write the **final thesis**; what you can do instead is to write a **working thesis**, a statement that you think will prove accurate.

Like any other sentence, a thesis consists of a **subject** and a **predicate**. The **subject** of your thesis should identify the subject of your essay. The **predicate** represents the claim (assertion) you want to make (see the diagram below):

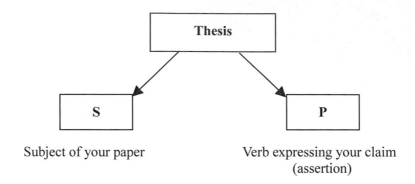

Subject of your paper   Verb expressing your claim
(assertion)

If we consider the thesis "*Watching TV has more advantages than disadvantages*", its **subject** is *"watching TV"*, while its predicate *"has more advantages than disadvantages"* will represent the claim (assertion) made by the writer.

 9 *Look at these thesis statements. Write their component parts in the table below:*

1. Printed media will soon be replaced by electronic media.
2. The monologue technique plays an important part in the dramatic development of Tennessee Williams' plays.
3. Efficient learners use various ways to improve their English speaking skills.

	Subject	**Claim**
1.		
2.		
3.		

Note that a thesis is **not** a simple statement of fact. Facts need not call for an opinion and arguments – investigation can prove whether they are true or false. A thesis statement, on the other hand, calls for your opinion. As shown above it represents your controlling idea and as such it requires you to make a judgment, take a stand, give reasons.

Fact: During the past few years, robotic systems have been used on a wide scale in the automobile industry.

Thesis:	The wide use of robots in the automobile industry has more advantages than disadvantages.

The thesis statement should be *limited* and *specific*. You should avoid a thesis that is too broad and vague. One way of doing this is to pose the journalist' s questions: *who? what? when? where? which?*
In writing their thesis, writers may display different levels of commitment.

Commitment refers here to what you are willing to do in your paper. We can make an analogy between intellectual commitment and the number of stories in a building:

Consider the following topic: ***Robots - a Mixed Blessing?***

- The lowest level is that of *one-story commitment*. Such writers present only a collection of facts and figures. Readers, on the other hand, want to know how these facts and figures are brought together in a meaningful way. Their expectations are baffled by a writer who makes a one-story commitment, because such a writer makes no attempt to create meaning.

Illustration:
A one-story writer may produce a thesis like this one: "Robots are useful for humans." It is quite obvious that such a thesis does not meet the requirements of the task which asks the writer to make a judgment and take a stand.

- *A two–story commitment writer* will act as a thinker, i.e. s/he will reason with facts and make observations about them or based on them. Such a person will define, classify, explain, analyze in order to *argue* and *inform* the reader.

Illustration:
Someone making a two-story commitment to the topic presented above might write a thesis like this: "Although robots may be considered a 'mixed blessing', we must be aware that they are the way forward and we cannot progress without them."

- *A three-story commitment* signals the most ambitious commitment a writer can make. Besides addressing the specific requirements of the topic question, such a writer shows his willingness to take risks by expanding the scope of the paper. This can be done by introducing a tension built on opposing elements that are not obvious on a first reading of the topic.

? 10 *Try to write a thesis showing a three-story commitment to the topic* **Robots - a Mixed Blessing?** *Before doing this, read the title again and identify a tension that may not be apparent at first sight.*

? 11 *Below are two sets of theses. Decide whether each thesis in each set has a* **one- , two-,** *or* **three-story commitment.** *Place the number and letter corresponding to each thesis under the appropriate heading. N.B. You should have two theses in each column! Explain your choice.*

One-story commitment thesis	Two- story commitment thesis	Three- story commitment thesis

1. a. Educators can use violence on TV to make teenagers confront aggression in themselves and in their environment, thus breaking the cycle of violence in the real world.
1. b. Violence on TV is not good for teenagers.
1. c. Violence on TV affects and changes teenagers.

2. a. Satire in *Gulliver's Travels* is in fact directed towards Swift's contemporary England
2. b. *Gulliver's Travels* is a great book.
2. c. By making his main character embark on various ships, first as a surgeon and then as a captain, Swift ridicules the sea voyage and shipwreck themes that were fashionable in his time, while criticizing both the society of his time and general human flaws.

? 12 *Below you have two topics. For each of them, write three theses, showing a one- , two-, and three-story commitment:*
1. Why are some students afraid of speaking English?
2. The dragon in Chinese myths and legends.

BASIC RESEARCH SKILLS

Gathering Information
Gathering Data
Once you have formulated a hypothesis, start gathering information to support your ideas. No matter how good your writing skills are, your paper will not be successful if it does not contain the necessary information. The data you need can be gathered from various sources: books, reference materials, periodicals, audio-visual materials, surveys, interviews. Some sources are located in the library, while others are outside the library.

Library Revisited
The chapter "Study Aids" familiarized you with various types of sources that can be found in a library. If you need to write a research paper, you should know more about the organization of your university or department library in order to be able to find the materials you need.

? **1** *Which are the main sections in your university/department library? Write them down in the spaces provided. If you don't know for sure, pay a visit to your library.*

_____

_____

_____

_____

Most libraries are divided into two main sections:
- the general circulation section
- the reference section

The *general circulation section* contains books and other materials that can be checked out and taken at home for a certain period of time stipulated in the library regulations.
The *reference section* includes reference books and periodicals that cannot be checked out and must be used within the library.

? **2** *Give examples of five types of reference books and three types of periodicals that are usually found in a library.*

Reference books

  1. _____

  2. _____

  3. _____

  4. _____

  5. _____

Periodicals

  1. _____

  2. _____

  3. _____

At the front of the library you can find the *circulation desk*. Here specialized personnel and/or students can help you find your way through the library or find whether the book you need is available or not. If the book you need is checked out, you can place a hold order and you will be contacted when the book is returned. If the material you need cannot be found in your university library, ask the personnel at the circulation desk to help you borrow it from another library through the *interlibrary loan service*.

The Library Catalog

Your key to finding materials in the library is the library catalog, which records all the books and other materials that it contains and gives the location of the respective source in the library. Traditionally, the library catalog consisted of many cards stored in alphabetical order according to the main author's last name in special cabinet drawers.

Public Access Catalog (PAC)

Most libraries have converted their card catalog into a computer version, called *Public Access Catalog* that lists books, video tapes, CDs or DVDs. If the process is not complete yet, some of the older books can be accessible only through the traditional *card files*. Whether on-line or on cards, an item is classified in three ways:

- by author
- by title
- by subject

Call Numbers

Libraries have many books. All of them need to be classified and arranged on shelves in a certain order. This is done by means of *call numbers* which classify books according to their subject area. The call number for each book appears in the card catalogue as part of the entry and also on the spine of the book. The call number is like an address that tells you where in the library you can find a certain book.

Most libraries use the Dewey Decimal Classification System for books call numbers. In this system, books are numbered according to ten main classes of subject areas:

000-099 General works (encyclopedias, bibliographies, periodicals)
100-199 Philosophy and related fields (psychology, logic, ethics)
200-299 Religion
300-399 Social sciences (political science, economics, law)
400-499 Language (dictionaries, grammar)
500-599 Pure sciences (mathematics, physics, chemistry, biology)
600-699 Technology (medicine, engineering, agriculture, business)
700-799 The arts (architecture, sculpture, painting, music)
800-899 Literature (novels, plays, poetry)
900-999 History and geography

Each class is then further subdivided into subclasses. Decimal numbers ensure further breakdowns of subject areas.

 3 *1. Choose one of the following topics:*

- English Drama in the 19th Century
- Shakespeare's Imagery
- French Impressionism
- Ancient Egypt
- How to Improve Your English Conversation Skills
- Varieties of English
- English as an International Language

2. Visit the university library and find as many sources on the topic chosen as you can. Look for books, reference materials, periodicals, as well as audio and video material. Come with a list of sources. Include the following information:
- For books: author, title, publisher, year, ISBN, and the local call number
- For journals: author, title of article, journal title, date, ISSN
- For DVD's: name, year, call number

Tips for Evaluating Source Materials

Let us suppose you have already visited the library and have found a great number of potential sources of information. How do you decide which ones are useful for you without having to read all of them from cover to cover? Here are some elements you should take into account:

- *Publication date*. When you are looking for information about a subject area that is developing rapidly, such as computers, neuroscience or genetics, you need to find up-to-date information. On the other hand, if you are dealing with a historical topic, i.e. *America in the 1920's*, books and periodicals published in that very period will give you valuable information. Remember that the publication date can be found by looking at the copyright page.
- *Edition*. If a book has been published in more than one edition, it means it was well received by the public and, consequently, it is worth reading. You can find information about the number of editions published by looking at the copyright page. Try to find and read the latest edition of a book.
- *Authorship*. A book or article written by a well known author or an expert in the field can add valuable support to your research paper. Therefore, look first for sources of information written by authoritative voices in the field. How can you find out about the author's qualifications? By reading the introduction, blurb or the book jacket.
- *Coverage*. Browse through the index and the table of contents to see how many pages are devoted to your topic. If it is only half a page, you should probably discard that source and look for others. If the topic is covered in several pages or a chapter, it is probably worth checking.
- *Difficulty*. If the information included is too difficult for you to understand and/or if the language is too technical or specialized, then you should probably look for another book.

Using Sources

In order to support your hypothesis, you need to document it by using sources. To be able to document your research, justify it and support your ideas, you first have to **critically** read sources and take notes.

Such reading is usually conducted at four levels or stages, each with its specific goals.

4 *Below are the four stages of reading (numbered 1-4) and the goals (a-d). Match each stage with its appropriate goal.*

Stage	Goals
1. Reading to understand	a) to determine the reliability of sources, by separating *fact* from *opinion* and by assessing the author's ideas and the evidence given.
2. Reading to respond	b) to read your sources carefully enough to be able to *react*, to *ask questions*, and to *find differences* between them.
3. Reading to evaluate	c) to determine how ideas in one source are related to ideas in other sources
4.Reading to synthesize	d) to familiarize yourself with your sources and determine their *relevance*.

Which of these levels of reading do you generally cover
a) when you write a research paper or a report?
b) when you prepare for your exams?

Creating a Bibliography
Definition: What?
What is a bibliography?

 5 *Complete the following definition:*

A bibliography is _____

_____

Now read your definition to your partner. Are your definitions similar or different?

To put it simply, the *bibliography* is a list of materials or sources of information for your topic.

When writing a research report, or any other text in which you quote sources, you need to create a bibliography. In fact, you will probably end up by having two versions of your bibliography:

- **a working bibliography**, which includes all the materials you found and read in preparing your paper;
- **a final bibliography** based on the former, which consists of those sources that you actually *use* in writing the paper.

Tips for Creating a Working Bibliography:

- Prepare your working bibliography *while* you are reading your sources (not afterwards). This way you can easily transfer the information you need on to your final bibliography. If you leave this activity to the last stages, or if you simply ignore having a working bibliography, you may have problems in devising your final bibliography, simply because you may have returned some materials and you do not have all the information about author, title, year of publication or volume.
- Use *bibliographic/source cards* to compile your working bibliography. These are small cards (approx. 8cm by 12cm) that allow you to easily alphabetize entries or to arrange them in any order you want (topic, subtopic).
- On your bibliographic card, record the following information:

For a book

1. **name of author** (last name first)/**name of editor** in case the book is a collection of articles
2. **title** (and subtitle)
3. **publication data:**
   a. place of publication
   b. name of publisher
   c. date of publication (consult the copyright page)
4. **number of pages**
5. Give a **code name/number** to each bibliographic entry. When you take notes on that source, it is easier to use that code, rather than write all the bibliographic information.

Illustration:

```
                                              ⎛ 3 ⎞
   Lester, James D.
   Writing Research Papers  (9ᵗʰ
   Edition)
   New York: Longman, 1998
   386 pp.
```

For a journal article:

1. **name of author** (last name first)
2. **title of article** (including subtitle)
3. **publication data:**
   a. name of journal
   b. volume number

c.date of issue

d.page numbers for the article (first page number and last page number)

Illustration:

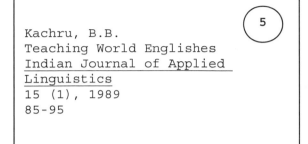

```
Kachru, B.B.                          5
Teaching World Englishes
Indian Journal of Applied
Linguistics
15 (1), 1989
85-95
```

? **6** *Find a book and an article **about** Shakespeare's plays. Write a bibliographic card for each of these two sources. You may need to go to the library to find these sources. Alternatively, you might search the internet.*

Making Handwritten Note Cards

Just like bibliographical cards, note cards are easy to be sorted out and rearranged as you wish.

You could use various formats for note cards, but there are some essential elements you should include:

- a **code number** similar to the code number on the bibliographic card/ **a code name**
- the **topic** or **subtopic** label
- the **note** itself
- a **page reference**

Limit each card to a single point or example. By doing this, it will be easier for you to arrange your cards according to the plan or sketch of your paper.

Illustrations:

a.

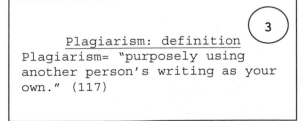

```
              Plagiarism: definition    3
Plagiarism= "purposely using
another person's writing as your
own." (117)
```

b.

```
                              Lester 117
            Plagiarism: definition
Plagiarism= "purposely using
another person's writing as your
own."
```

The former example used a *code number*, while the latter used a *code name*, i.e. the author's surname. It is written on the top right hand corner and is followed by the page number.

Tips for Handwritten Note Cards
- Take notes on one side of the card.
- Write in ink.
- Write only **one** item (quotation, fact, idea) on each card. This will help you arrange your cards in any way you want.
- Place the source code number in the upper right hand corner.
- Do not forget to write the source page number.
- Write a label (headline) that identifies the topic/subtopic the note refers to. This will make it easier for you to group together cards dealing with the same topic/subtopic.

Making Notes on Your Computer
If you prefer to make your notes using a computer, you can do it in several ways:

1. You can use *Word* to write your notes
   a. as separate files under one common directory
      - first create a directory and give it a name
      - then create various files for your notes and give each of them a specific name
   b. as a single file
      - create a file and give it a name
      - write all your notes in this file, giving each a code number or a code word
2. You can use Power Point to write your notes. In this case, each slide will look like a handwritten note card, i.e. each slide will contain **one** item and will be labeled.

Plagiarism: definition

◦ Plagiarism= "purposely using another person's writing as your own." (117)

Types of Notes Used for Research Papers

Your research paper has to be well documented with ideas, facts and figures, details and examples that support your hypothesis. When reading sources or when thinking about your topic, you should make notes either on note cards or in your computer files. These notes fall under the following headings:

- Quotations
- Summary notes
- Paraphrases
- Personal notes

Quotations
Definition

A *quotation* or *quote* is the exact rendering of a source passage. This means that when you write a quotation you must give the author's exact words and use his/her exact punctuation. There are three main situations in which you should quote:

- when you want to support your ideas and enhance your credibility by drawing on the words of an authority on that subject;
- when, on the contrary, you want to discredit an idea from a certain source;
- when the language of the source is particularly effective.

Characteristics of Quotes

- Quotations must be placed between quotation marks (" ")
- The source must be acknowledged (author, page number) in the so called in-text citation. This can be structured in two main ways:

    a. *quotation* followed by *author's surname* and *page* (the last two are placed in brackets)

Illustration:

"A text can be defined as an actual use of language, as distinct from a sentence which is an abstract unit of linguistic analysis" (Widdowson 4).

    b. *author's surname* followed by *quotation* and *page* (this one placed in brackets)

Illustration:

Widdowson sees a text as "an actual use of language, as distinct from a sentence which is an abstract unit of linguistic analysis" (4).

- What is in the brackets after the quotation goes *outside* the quotation marks, but *inside* the period.
- Quotations should be short. Do *not* use long quotes.

To quote means to give an author's exact words using the same punctuation as in the original. However, there are certain situations in which you may need to make *small additions*, some *capitalization changes* or *omissions* to quotations for the sake of clarity, conciseness or smoothness.

Additions/ Small Changes
If you need to *add* or *replace* some words in a passage you quote, you should place the words you add in *square brackets* [ ].

Illustration
Original Passage
"He has distinguished himself not merely by his prodigious output as a physicist - notably by his contribution to the unification of the weak and electromagnetic interactions - but also for his careful and scholarly approach to popularizing physics."

Quotation
"[Steven Weinberg] has distinguished himself not merely by his prodigious output as a physicist - notably by his contribution to the unification of the weak and electromagnetic interactions - but also for his careful and scholarly approach to popularizing physics."

If you need to *change* a capital letter to a lowercase one in order to integrate the quotation in your sentence, place the lowercase letter in *square brackets* [ ].

Illustration
Original Passage
"The branch of engineering concerned with the presentation of measured data at a location remote from the source of the data."

Quotation
John Truxal defines telemetering as "[t]he branch of engineering concerned with the presentation of measured data at a location remote from the source of the data."

Omissions
If you want to omit something from the original source when quoting you can use an *ellipsis* – three spaced dots:

Illustration
Original Passage
"The term electrical telemetry is utilized in contrast to radio telemetry and refers to wired telemetry systems in which the information is transmitted by variations of a voltage or current in the electric circuit."

Quotation
"The term electrical telemetry... refers to wired telemetry systems in which the information is transmitted by variations of a voltage or current in the electric circuit."

Introducing Quotations
Quoted sentences are introduced by **attributive phrases**:
- according to
- as X argues/claims/points out

Verbs that introduce quotations are:

add	compare	emphasize	report
agree	conclude	explain	say
argue	consider	find	see
ask	declare	note	show
believe	deny	observe	suggest
claim	disagree	relate	think

When you quote a longer passage (say longer than four lines), you should use a *block quotation*, i.e. set the passage apart from the text, by indenting it. You need not place *block quotations* between quotation marks.

Illustration:
Speaking about Hamlet's personality, Mangan shows that

> [i]t is a common obsession of Hamlet throughout the play that he is always looking for some sort of truth that exists beneath the surface of things…He has, in effect, split himself into two parts: there is the outer self, which is for public consumption. He happens to want to communicate his feelings, and so he wears black and moons about sullenly; but, he implies, it would be just as easy for him to 'play a part' and conceal those feelings – just as it would be possible for someone who did *not* feel grief to play the part of a mourner (125).

However, you should avoid using long or too many quotations in your paper because this might mean that you have little to say on the subject. Remember that one of the purposes of a research paper is to demonstrate that you can 'digest' and evaluate the information from sources and that you can express your own ideas. If the proportion of quotations in your paper is 10% to 15%, it is already too much. One way of avoiding using too many quotations or quotations that are too long is to write *summary notes*.

Summary Notes

?7 *What is a summary? Which are its characteristics? Complete the sentences below. Remember that there is a special chapter on summarizing in this book.*

A summary is_____

_____

Characteristics of an effective summary:

_____

_____

_____

_____

_____

_____

_____

_____

You can write summarize different ideas from books or articles on your note cards. For example, the longer quotation about Hamlet's personality above could be summarized in a few words on a note card.

Illustration:

```
                                    Mangan 125
              Hamlet as a character
Hamlet's   personality   is   split
between  the  inner  and  the  outer
self.
```

Notice that when you write summary notes **you should** also acknowledge the **source** (author and page), just as in the case of quotations. This is because the ideas in the summary belong to someone else. In the case of summary notes, however, you **should not use quotation marks**, because you do not use the author's exact words.

If you incorporate the previous summary notes into your paper, you may obtain something like:

Mangan considers that a characteristic of Hamlet's personality is the split between the inner and the outer self (125).

?8 *Check your understanding of the previous passage. Write T if you think the statement is correct and F if you think it is false.*

1. ___When you summarize another author's ideas in your own words you should put the summary between quotation marks.
2. ___If you summarize ideas found in a book or article, you should mention the author's name and the page.

Paraphrases

Definition

A **paraphrase** is a restatement, or reformulation, in your own words, of a passage of text. Unlike the summary, a paraphrase is usually about the same length as the original and it follows more closely the order of ideas, meaning, tone, and key words of the passage.

The length of a paraphrase depends on your purpose and on the density of information in the source passage.

SPA

- The subject is that of the material you are paraphrasing (passage from a book, an article, etc)
- The *purpose* is twofold:
  - to clarify/explain complex ideas/difficult terminology in a short passage
  - to present all the (major and minor) points in the original in your own words
- The intended *reader* may be
  - the teacher (when you are asked to write a paraphrase as part of your coursework or to paraphrase sources in your research paper)
  - any reader of a certain publication/ any internet surfer (when your paper with paraphrases from various sources appears in printed/ electronic media)

Paraphrase and Summary

- There are two main *similarities* between a paraphrase and a summary:
  1. Just like a summary, a paraphrase is a *secondary type of writing*, i.e. the ideas in the paraphrase belong to the source material, not to the writer of the paraphrase.
  2. Like a summary, a paraphrase is made up of complete sentences that are connected to a certain topic.

- There are several *differences* between a paraphrase and a summary:
  1. Unlike a summary, a paraphrase is about the same length as the original
  2. A paraphrase follows more closely the main points, the tone and the key vocabulary in the original passage.
  3. Besides *restating* the ideas in the original, a paraphrase also *clarifies*, *explains* or *interprets* the meaning of the source passage, thus acting as a bridge between the source text and the reader.

Illustration:

The longer quotation about Hamlet can be paraphrased as:

```
                                     Mangan 125
           Hamlet as a character
Hamlet is searching for the truth that lies
beyond the mere appearance of things. His own
personality is split between the 'inner
self', the true being, and the 'outer self ',
which is destined for "public consumption."
The outer self can be true to the inner self
or it can be just a mask.
```

This paraphrase note can then be inserted in your paper as:

Mangan regards Hamlet as a character who is searching for the truth that lies beyond the mere appearance of things. He argues that Hamlet's personality is split between the 'inner self', the true being, and the 'outer self ', which is destined for "public consumption." The outer self can be true to the inner self or it can be just a mask. (125).

Tips for Writing a Paraphrase

- Your paraphrase should be about the same length as the original passage
- Cite the source (the author and page number).
- Insert key words or phrases from the original by placing them between quotation marks (see example above)
- Preserve the same tone as that of the original passage (satiric, serious, friendly, patronizing, formal/informal, neutral, self-mocking, gentle, etc)
- Introduce the paraphrase with appropriate verbs (see the verbs mentioned for quotations)

? 9 *Use the information in this chapter and place a tick (√) in the appropriate column when the characteristic applies.*

	Length			Choice of words		
	Much shorter than the source passage	About as long as the source passage	As long as the source passage	Exact words as in the source	Your own words	Your own words and some key words
summary						
paraphrase						
quotation						

? 10 *Read the note cards below and decide which is a quotation, which is a summary and which is a paraphrase. Put quotation marks at the beginning and at the end of the quotation card.*

1. ☐

> Truxal 319
>
> *Telemetering*
> Telemetering or telemetry is a "branch of engineering concerned with the presentation of measured data at a location remote from the source of the data." It includes all remote metering, no matter whether the distance is small or great. Its functions are threefold: the generation of a signal meant to measure the physical variable; the transmission of that signal to the remote location and the conversion of the data into a form that can be displayed, recorded or applied to further data-processing equipment.

2. ☐

```
                                                          Truxal 319
                           Telemetering
The  branch  of  engineering  concerned  with  the  presentation  of
measured data at a location remote from the source of the data; also
called   telemetry.   Telemetry   encompasses   all   remote  metering,
whether the distances involved be many miles, as in space flights,
or only a few feet, as in the measurement of reactivity in the core
of a nuclear reactor.
Telemetry involves three separate functions: (1) generation of a
signal (electrical or otherwise), which measures the pertinent
physical variable and is in suitable form for transmission; (2)
transmission of the information to the remote location; and (3)
conversion  of  the  data  into  a  form  appropriate  for  display,
recording, or application for further data processing equipment.
```

3. ☐

```
                                                          Truxal 319

                           Telemetering
Telemetering, or telemetry, which refers to anything that involves
remote metering, has three distinct functions: the generation of a
signal meant to measure the physical variable, the sending of that
signal to the remote location and the conversion of the information
into a manageable form.
```

Plagiarism: Definition

Plagiarism means copying someone else's words or ideas and presenting them as your own, without acknowledging the source. The term comes from the Latin word *plagiarius*, meaning 'kidnapper.' It is a kind of theft, an *intellectual theft*, because a plagiarist *steals* or '*kidnaps*' another person's ideas and/or words.

Plagiarism is considered a moral and ethical offence. Students who commit plagiarism in their assignments or research papers usually fail the course or may even be expelled from school or university.

146

? 11 *How do students feel about plagiarism in your culture? How is this offence usually penalized?*

In some cultures, there is a high respect for the words and teachings attributed to great scholars. This does not mean, however, that people who belong to such a culture can use those words and ideas as their own, because doing that is an offence.

However, you can 'borrow' without having to acknowledge the following:

- Well-known proverbs: "A friend in need is a friend indeed."
- General/common knowledge: Paris is the capital of France.

How to Avoid Plagiarism?

Plagiarism can be easily avoided:

- Place all quoted materials within quotation marks.
- If you paraphrase or summarize a source, make sure you rewrite materials in your own words.
- Acknowledge the source by providing in-text citations (author, page) and by including the source material in your *Bibliography*, *References* or *Works Cited* list.

Illustration:

Original Source

"The opening scene of *King Lear* bears a structural similarity to Act I, Scene ii of *Hamlet*. Both are occasions of a royal proclamation and state ceremony – and are in fact mirror images of each other in this respect. (Michael Mangan, "A Preface to Shakespeare's Tragedies" [London: Longman, 1991] 166).

Version A: Plagiarism

There is a great similarity between the first scene in *King Lear* and the second scene in the first act of *Hamlet*. These scenes can be said to be mirror images, because in both of them we can see a royal proclamation made in front of the court.

Version A is an instance of plagiarism, because here the writer has borrowed from the original source without documenting it (there are no references to the original source).

Version B: Acceptable

According to Michael Mangan, the first scene in *King Lear* is structurally similar to the second scene in the opening act of *Hamlet*. Mangan claims these two scenes can be considered "mirror images", as they both present a declaration of the king made in front of the court (166).

CREATING A BIBLIOGRAPHY

MLA Style

The sources you quote from, paraphrase, summarize or refer to should be acknowledged both *in the text* of the paper or report as such and at the end, in a special section.

Although the content is pretty much the same, there are certain differences in the conventions of style regarding the sequencing of items in a bibliography, depending on the field of study: humanities, social sciences, sciences.

The style followed here is the one suggested by the **Modern Language Association (MLA),** an organization made up of college English and foreign language teachers.

Format

1. Type your bibliographic list on a computer.
2. Select one of the following headings for your bibliographic list:
   - *Works Cited.* Choose this heading in case your list includes only the printed works that were quoted, paraphrased or summarized in your paper.
   - *Sources Cited.* Select this heading if your list includes printed works as well as non print sources (Internet materials, films, video clips, interviews).
   - *Bibliography.* Opt for this heading if you give a *complete* list of *all* works related to the subject. As an undergraduate student, you probably need not do that, so at this stage, you are more likely to select one of the first two options.
3. Start your bibliographic list on a new page *after* the main body of your paper.
4. Leave one-inch margins on each side (top, bottom, right, left)
5. Center the heading *Works Cited/Sources Cited* and place it at one inch from the top of the page.
6. Double space between the heading and the first entry, as well as between and within the entries.
7. Place entries in alphabetical order by author's surname.
8. Write the first line of each entry flush with the left hand margin.
9. If an entry runs more than one line, indent all the additional lines five spaces (or a tab).
10. Place your surname and the page number one-half inch from the top in the upper right-hand corner. This page number should continue the numbering from the text.

Brown 15

Works Cited

Allwright, R. L. "Classroom-Centered Research on Language Teaching and Learning: A Brief Historical Overview." <u>TESOL Quarterly</u> 17 (1983): 191-204.

---. <u>Observation in the Language Classroom</u>. London: Longman, 1988.

Bailey, Kathleen M. "Competitiveness and Anxiety in Adult Second Language Learning: Looking *at* and *through* the Diary Studies." <u>Classroom Oriented Research in Second Language Acquisition</u>. Eds. H. Selinger and M. Long. Rowley, MA: Newbury, 1983. 67-103.

Bailey, Kenneth D. <u>Methods of Social Research</u>. 2nd ed. New York: Macmillan, 1981.

Chaudron, Craig, and Jack C. Richards. "The Effect of Discourse Markers on the Comprehension of Lectures." <u>Applied Linguistics</u> 7 (1986): 113-27.

? 1. *Have a look at the "Works Cited" list and answer the following questions:*

1. How are the entries ordered?
2. In the list there are two authors with the same surname, i.e. Bailey. Why do you think Kathleen Bailey appears *before* Kenneth Bailey? Try to formulate a rule.
3. Why does "Classroom-Centered Research on Language Teaching and Learning" appear *before* <u>Observation in the Language Classroom</u>?

Ordering Entries
There are some conventions regarding the order of entries that should be observed.
- Items should be placed in alphabetical order by author's surname. This means that the author's name appears in the order *surname + first name + middle name*.
- If there are two or more authors with the same surname, list them according to the alphabetic order of their *first names*, as in this example:
  Bailey, Kathleen M
  Bailey, Kenneth D
- If there are two or more works by the same writer, place them in the alphabetic order of their title.

Entry in MLA Style
In MLA style there are variations in the entry structure, depending on whether you enter information about a book, a printed article, an electronic source or other materials.

Book Entry in MLA Style
Below are the possible items of a book entry and the order in which they appear:
1. **Author(s)**
2. Title of chapter/part of a book
3. **Title of book**
4. Name of editor or translator
5. Edition
6. Volume number
7. **Publication information**
   - **Place**
   - **Publisher**
   - **Date**
8. Page numbers

Out of these elements, the items in bold (1, 3, and 7) are compulsory for all book entries. The others will be enlisted in case the book displays those features.
Let us now have a closer look at the basic book entry:
The basic book entry is made up of three main parts:
1. Author's name (last, first middle)
2. Title of the book
3. Publication information (place, publisher, and date)
In your bibliographic form, these three parts will be separated by periods:

> Author's Surname, Author's First name Author's Middle Name. Book Title. Place:
>
> Publisher, date.

Illustration:
Bevis, Richard W. English Drama: Restoration and the Eighteenth Century, 1660-1789.

London: Longman, 1988.

Author(s)

?2 *Have a look at the "Works Cited" list below and answer the following questions:*
1. Look at the entry with Kathleen Bailey. What punctuation mark is used between the author's surname and her first name? What punctuation mark is used after the author's complete name?

2. Look at the last entry. The first author's name appears in the order surname + first name. What about the second author's name?
3. Which book has three authors? How are their names written?
4. Who wrote "Turns, Topics, and Tasks: Patterns of Participation in Language Learning and Teaching"? What appears in the list instead of the author's name?
5. Who are the editors of <u>Voices from the Language Classroom?</u>

Works Cited

Allwright, R. L. <u>Observation in the Language Classroom</u>. London: Longman, 1988.

---."Turns, Topics, and Tasks: Patterns of Participation in Language Learning and Teaching." <u>Discourse Analysis in Second Language Research</u>. Ed. Diane Larsen-Freeman. Rowley, MA: Newbury, 1980. 165-87.

Altrichter, Herbert, Peter Posch, and Bridget Somekh. <u>Teachers Investigate Their Work: An Introduction to the Methods of Action Research</u>. London: Routledge, 1993.

Bailey, Kathleen M. "Competitiveness and Anxiety in Adult Second Language Learning: Looking *at* and *through* the Diary Studies." <u>Classroom Oriented Research in Second Language Acquisition</u>. Eds. H. Selinger and M. Long. Rowley, MA: Newbury, 1983. 67-103.

---. <u>Language Teacher Supervision</u>. Cambridge: Cambridge UP, 2006.

---, and David Nunan, eds. <u>Voices from the Language Classroom</u>. Cambridge: Cambridge UP, 1996.

Chaudron, Craig, and Jack C. Richards. "The Effect of Discourse Markers on the Comprehension of Lectures." <u>Applied Linguistics</u> 7 (1986): 113-27.

Some Tips
- The author's name appears in reverse order (last, first middle)
- Place a comma after the last name (Bevis, Richard) and a period at the end of the name

Last Name, First Name Middle Name.

Illustration:

> Bevis, Richard W.

- If there is more than one author, the first author's name will appear in the order indicated above (*surname, first name middle name*); the names of the other authors will appear in the order *first name middle name surname*. Between the names of two different authors there will be a comma; the last author's name is preceded by *and*.

Illustration:

> Chaudron, Craig, and Jack C. Richards.
> Altrichter, Herbert, Peter Posch, and Bridget Somekh.

- If your list includes two or more works by the same writer, give the name of the writer only in the first entry. For the other entries substitute the name by three hyphens followed by a period (---.)

Illustration:

> Bailey, Kathleen M.
> ---.

- Give the author's name in full if it appears in full on the title page and use initials for the first and/or middle names if such initials are used on the title page.
- Omit titles or degrees that accompany names.

Illustration:

Title Page	Works/Sources Cited
David Nunan	Nunan, David.
Kathleen M. Bailey	Bailey, Kathleen M.
Sir Robert Louis Stevenson	Stevenson, Robert Louis.

?3 *Below are some entries from a bibliographic list. Put them in the proper order, by placing numbers in front of each. Make any necessary alterations.*

Works Cited

Kempe, Andy, and Lionel Warner. <u>Starting with Scripts</u>. Cheltenham: Nelson Thornes, 2002.

Chen, Jin-Fen. <u>English Teaching Materials and Methods of Elementary School-The Potential and Consideration of Multimedia in English Teaching.</u> Taipei: Crane, 1999.

Baldwin, Patrice, and Kate Fleming. <u>Teaching Literacy through Drama</u>. New York: Routledge, 2003.

Kempe, Andy. "Reading Plays for Performance." <u>On the Subjects of Drama</u>. Ed. David Hornbrook. New York: Routledge, 1998.

Chen, Chi-Lie. <u>Aboriginal Education in Taiwan</u>. Taipei: Shi-Da, 1997.

Carter, Ronald, and Michael N. Long. <u>Teaching Literature</u>. Harlow: Longman, 1991.

Book Title
- Write the full title of the book, including any subtitle
- Place a colon between the title and the subtitle and a period at the end of the full title
- Underline the title (but do not underline the period at the end). Alternatively, you can use *italics.*
- Capitalize all the principal words in the title:
  -nouns
  -pronouns
  -adjectives
  -adverbs
  -verbs

Chaudron, Craig. <u>Second Language Classrooms: Research on Teaching and Learning</u>.
  or
Chaudron, Craig. *Second Language Classrooms: Research on Teaching and Learning.*

Publication Information
- The order of this information is:

Place: Publisher, date

- The place of publication is the city where the book was published: New York, London, Taipei, Paris, etc. This information can be taken from the title page or from the copyright page.

- If more than one city is listed on the copyright page, use only the *first* city given for the bibliographic list.
- Place a colon between the place and the publisher.
- Place a comma between the publisher and the date.
- Place a period after the date.
- Shorten the publisher's name:
  -Omit - articles (a, an, the)
  - business abbreviations (Co., Corp., Inc., Ltd.)
  - descriptive words (Books, House, Press, Publishers)
  -For University Press, use the abbreviation UP (Cambridge UP)
- If the date does not appear on the title page, use the most recent copyright date. You can find it on the copyright page after the sign ©.
- If the book has been reprinted by the same editor, use the original publication date.

Other Items

Title of Chapter/Part of a Book

If in your paper you quote from one work (e.g. a chapter) in a collection of chapters written by different authors, your entry will include the following elements:

1. Author's name (last, first, middle), followed by a period.
2. The title of the chapter or part of that book between quotation marks.
3. The title of the book (underlined or in italics), followed by a period.
4. The abbreviation *Ed.* (editor), or *Eds.* (editors), followed by the name(s) of the editor(s), in the order *first name last name*. Place a period after the name of the editor.
5. Publication information (Place: Publisher, date), followed by a period.
6. Pages (e.g. 55-70), followed by a period.

Author's Last Name, Author's First Name Author's Middle Name. "Title of Chapter."

Title of Book. Ed. First Name Last Name. Place: Publisher, date. Pages.

Illustration:

Greenblatt, Stephen. "The Improvisation of Power." Shakespearean Tragedy. Ed. John

Drakakis. Harlow: Longman Pearson, 1992. 153-193.

Editor/Translator

As shown above, the name of the editor or of the translator will be preceded by the abbreviation *Ed.* or *Trans.* and will be placed *between* the title of the book and the place of publication.

Volume
If a book has several volumes and you cite only one volume, provide the volume number just *before* the place of publication.

Illustration:
Hume, David. <u>The History of England</u>. Vol. 2. Indianapolis: Liberty Fund, 1983.

Entries for Periodicals in MLA Style
Journals

 4 *Have a look at the journal entries below.*

The last entry introduces an article that was published in <u>Language Learning</u>, Volume 55, Number 3, pages 410 to 439. Notice that the words *volume*, *issue* and *pages* are omitted from the entry.

Now have another look at the entries and answer the following questions:
1. Which is the first element in all these entries? Does this element also appear first in book entries?
2. Who are the authors of the article on discourse markers? How are their names written?
3. What volume of <u>TESOL Quarterly</u> did Allwright's article appear in? On what pages?
4. What number in <u>Applied Linguistics</u> did Fung and Carter's article appear in?
5. What article did Allwright write? What punctuation marks appear at the beginning and at the end of the title?
6. What is the name of the journal in which the article on discourse markers appeared? How is this name written?

Works Cited

Allwright, R. "Classroom-Centered Research on Language Teaching and Learning: A Brief Historical Overview." <u>TESOL Quarterly</u>. 17 (1983): 191-204.

Fung, Loretta, and Ronald Carter. "Discourse Markers and Spoken English: Native and Learner Use in Pedagogic Settings." <u>Applied Linguistics</u>. 28.3 (2007): 410-39.

Gass, Susan, Alison Mackey, and Lauren-Ross Friedman. "Task-Based Interactions in Classroom and Laboratory Settings." <u>Language Learning</u>. 55.4 (2005): 575-611.

A journal entry in MLA style will use the following order:

1. Author's name
2. Title of the article
3. Publication information
   - Name of the journal
   - Volume number
   - Date of publication
4. Inclusive page numbers of the article

Author(s)

- Similar to book entries, place the author's name flush left in the order *last, first, middle name*. Put a period at the end of the author's name.
- If there are more authors, the order will be:
  - for the first author: *last,   first   middle name.*
  - for the other authors: *first   last   middle name.*

Illustration:

> Fung Loretta, and Ronald Carter.
> Gass, Susan, Alison Mackey, and Lauren-Ross Friedman.

Title of the Article

- Place the title of the article immediately *after* the author's name.
- Put the title between quotation marks, followed by a period *inside* the quotation marks.

Illustration:

> Ur, Penny. "Teacher Learning."

Publication information

Place this information in the order below:

- Journal Title. The journal title is underlined or in italics and is followed by a period.
- Volume number. Do *not* write the word *volume*; write only the its number, e.g. 15
- Date of publication. The date of publication is placed in brackets, e.g. (2001) and is followed by a colon, e.g. (2001):

Illustration:

> ELT Journal. 46 (1992):

- Take the publication information from the journal cover or from the title page.

Page Numbers
- The page numbers are the last element in your entry
- Insert the number corresponding to the first page of the article, put a hyphen and add the number of the last page of the article, followed by a period, e.g. 133-147.

Let us put all the elements together now:

Illustration:

Ur, Penny. "Teacher Learning." ELT Journal. 46 (1992): 56-61.

Newspapers
In order to write a newspaper entry in MLA style, include the following elements:
1. Author's name in reverse order (*last, first, middle*), followed by a period.
2. Title of the article between quotation marks, followed by a period *inside* the quotation marks.
3. Name of the newspaper (underlined), followed by a period. Omit any introductory articles from this name, e.g. Daily Telegraph, New York Times.
4. The complete date: day, month (abbreviated), year, followed by a colon, e.g. 2 Aug. 2007:
5. The page number.

Illustration:

Helm, Toby, and Rebecca Smith. "Pupils to Be Paid to Eat Healthy Food." Daily Telegraph. 16 Feb. 2008: 14.

Lin, Jerry. "USB Adds Two New Wealth Management Branches." Taipei Times. 15 April 2008: 12.

Electronic Sources
If you quote from an internet source, give the following information:
1. Author's name, followed by a period.
2. Title of the article between quotation marks.
3. Name of book, journal, newspaper, in italics.
4. Publication information (depending on the source), followed by a period.
5. Date of your access, followed by a period.
6. URL, between angle brackets < >.

Illustration

Hunt, Alan, and David Beglar. "A Framework for Developing EFL Reading Vocabulary." *Reading in a Foreign Language*. 17.1 (2005). 23 Jan. 2008.

< http://www.nflrc. hawaii.edu/rfl/April2005>.

PREPARING FOR EXAMS

Examinations represent an important part of a student's life. They are part of evaluation or assessment procedures that may also include projects, oral or written reports or essays or other kinds of written assignments.

?1 *Think about the exams you have to pass as a university student. Answer these questions.*

1. When are your exam periods?
2. Is your exams date a given, or can you discuss it and agree on it with your professors?
3. When do you start preparing for your exams? Check (√) what is true about you, trying to be as honest as possible.
   a. from the beginning of the semester
   b. a week before the exam date
   c. one or two days before
   d. the night before the exam
   e. you don't really prepare for exams
4. Do you feel anxiety and fear before exams?
5. If you feel anxiety before an exam, this happens because…. (Check what is true about you; you may choose more answers)
   a. you haven't prepared well enough
   b. you have unrealistic expectations of excellent achievement
   c. your parents expect you to take very high grades
   d. peer pressure deriving from competition
   e. you are afraid of failing the exam
   f. other reasons (please specify)
6. If you feel stress before an exam, how do you try to relieve it? Check what is true about you
   a. walking
   b. jogging
   c. doing sports activities, e.g. going to the gym, playing basketball
   d. watching TV

e. going to a movie theater

f. playing computer games

g. listening to music

h. karaoke

i. doing breathing exercises

j. going shopping

k. chatting with friends

l. chatting on the internet

m. other (please specify)

Some Tips for Exam Preparation

In a sense, preparation for an exam starts with the first class you attend in an academic year. This way you can take control of your studying and, as a consequence, you can build self confidence. Broadly speaking, the tips that follow can be grouped into two main categories: general preparation tips and specific preparation tips.

2 *Have a look at the following tips. Rank them in order of importance, 1 being the most important. You can give the same number to several items if you think they are equally important.*

General Preparation

    a. ___Concentrate in class

    b. ___Take good notes in class lectures and from textbooks

    c. ___Review your notes and materials shortly after class

    d. ___Review your notes and materials briefly before the next class

    e. ___Study a little every day, don't wait until the exam is near

    f. ___Schedule a longer reviewing session each week

Specific Preparation

    g. ___Be attentive to what the teacher tells you about the exam: materials to be studied, types of questions (comprehension, true-false, multiple-choice, etc).

    h. ___For each exam, break up your materials (from notes, textbooks) in units/chunks to be studied in one study session.

    i. ___Estimate how much time you have at your disposal.

    j. ___Devise a timetable for your exam preparation.

    k. ___Stick to the timetable you have devised.

    l. ___Study the most difficult materials when you are alert.

    m. ___Find a good place to study (quiet, well lit, no distractors).

n. ___Don't listen to other students panicking about the exam.

o. ___Use relaxation techniques to get rid of stress.

p. ___Finish studying the day before the exam. If you wish, you can schedule a general revision of the materials for this day.

q. ___Try to test yourself from the materials you have studied.

The day before the exam you should try to make a checklist of specific things you need to remember for the exam. In a way, it is like making a list of things you need to take when going on a trip.

? **3** *Here is a list of things you need to remember before an exam. Work with a partner to complete it.*

1. Check the exact time and place of the exam.
2. Take your ID.
3. _____
4. _____
5. _____

Coping with Stress

It is said that a little bit of pressure may have a positive influence on your studies and in preparing for an exam, because it may act as an incentive to learning. A great amount of pressure or anxiety, however, can create big problems because it can interfere in a negative way with your learning.

So, how can you reduce anxiety? How can you cope with stress?

? **4** *Here you can find advice on how to reduce test or exam anxiety. Discuss these suggestions in groups of 3 or 4 students. Which of them do you already use? Which of them would you like to try in the future? Would you like to add any others to the list?*

Before the Exam Period

a. Take control of your study (see previous tips).
b. Build your self confidence.
c. Be well prepared for the exam.

d. Have a positive attitude. See the exam as an opportunity to show how much you have studied.

e. Use relaxation techniques to relieve stress: have a walk, watch TV, listen to music, practice sports, etc.

f. Avoid speaking with classmates who have not prepared and may express negative feelings.

The Day Before the Exam

g. Allow time for relaxation: go for a walk, watch a movie, chat with friends, etc.

h. Have a good night's sleep before the exam.

During the Exam

i. Try to feel relaxed. If you feel anxiety, pause and take a deep breath.

j. Don't think about the fear. Just take the exam questions step by step.

k. Don't panic if you see other students handing in their papers. Finishing earlier does not necessarily mean writing a good paper.

Some Tips for Success in Exams

5 *Here are some true and false assumptions about good performance during an exam. Work with a partner.*

First match each tip in part A with its counterpart in B, by completing the diagram below. Then, for each pair, decide which the real tip is.

A	B
1	
2	
3	
4	
5	

Real tips: ___, ___, ___, ___, ___.

A.

1. Arrive earlier so that you can find your seat easily, and prepare your pens and pencils before the teacher comes.

2. There is no need to read the directions for each section of the test if you listen to what the teacher says.

3. In a written exam, answer the questions in a strategic order: start with the easy questions first in order to boost your confidence and score points; continue with the more difficult ones or the ones that are worth more points.
4. If most of the other students have finished, it means you should finish, too. You don't want to be the last one to hand in the paper, do you?
5. Leave the exam room as soon as you have completed all the items.

B.
   a. Read the directions carefully. They will help you to avoid errors.
   b. After you have completed the test, allow at least 10 minutes to review and, if necessary, correct your answers.
   c. You should not panic if other students have handed in their papers, and there is still time. The important thing is to make sure you have written a good exam paper.
   d. There is no need for you to come earlier for the exam. Just be on time – don't be late.
   e. You should always answer the test questions in the order in which they appear on the question sheet.

Common Types of Questions in a Written Examination
True/False

Such test items include several statements that need to be labeled either T (true) or F (false).

True/ false items may test your knowledge of the materials studied:

Illustration:

 6 *Below are some tips on what you should/shouldn't do when writing your CV. On your answer sheet, write T if you think the statement is true and F if you think the statement is false.*

1. Your CV should be handwritten.
2. A CV should be short.
3. A CV should have a clear layout.
4. Abbreviations should be used.
5. Work experience should be listed in reverse chronology.
6. You shouldn't lie about your qualifications.
7. You should include all your hobbies.
8. You shouldn't use the pronoun "I" a lot.
9. You should use brightly colored paper.
10. Your CV should be adapted to the job you are applying for.

True/ false items may also test your comprehension of a new text during a reading exam:

Illustration:

Read the following passage and determine whether the following statements are TRUE (T) or FALSE (F).
1. The majority of children in Britain attend private schools.
2. Compulsory education in Britain is from the age of 5 to 16.
3. Schools are generally classified according to the type of education and the pupils' age.
4. In Britain there are three main types of schools: primary, secondary and high schools.
5. Primary school children are generally aged between 7 and 10 years old.
6. Children aged 5 to 7 years old attend infant schools.
7. Older primary school children (aged 7-11) attend junior schools.
8. Secondary school children normally attend comprehensive schools.
9. At 16 some pupils leave school.
10. After 16, some pupils stay on at school for four more years.

Tips for True/False Tests
- A true/false statement is considered true only if every part of the sentence is true. For example, the sentence "The thesis statement is usually the first sentence in the introduction" should be considered *false*, because, although part of it is true (the thesis is in the introduction), it is not *completely true* (the thesis is normally at the end of the introduction).
- If the statement is a long sentence, pay attention to the truth of each part. If one part is false, it usually means the whole statement is false.
- Negatives (*not, no*) can be confusing or misleading. If you are not sure whether a negative sentence is true or false, make it affirmative. If the corresponding affirmative sentence is true, then the initial sentence (the negative one) will be false.

Multiple-Choice
These tests consist either of a question or an incomplete sentence that you have to answer/complete by choosing the best response from a list of three to five options.

 *You have five minutes to complete this test. Circle the correct answer:*
1. Polygraphs record changes in _____
   a. body temperature and blood pressure.
   b. brain activity, blood pressure and arm movement.
   c. breathing and eye contact.
   d. breathing, heart rate and perspiration.

2. Which of these is not a characteristic of prescriptive grammars?
   a. They describe in an objective way the rules native speakers seem to follow.
   b. They prescribe rules of correct usage.
   c. They state that English sentences should not end in prepositions.
   d. They are against regionalisms and contractions that do not follow rules.

3. Which of the following can be protected by a patent?
   a. a new species of insects
   b. a new species of plants
   c. a new device or machinery
   d. a new planet

4. Which of these statements is false?
   a. Brazil is made up of 26 states and one federal district.
   b. Brazil's capital is Brasilia.
   c. The official language of Brazil is Spanish.
   d. The world famous carnival in Rio de Janeiro is held 40 days before Easter.

Statistics show that the chances of answering correctly by guessing in a multiple-choice test are of 20%. The best way to raise this percentage is to study. When faced with a multiple-choice test, students also apply some strategies that help them increase their scores.

8 *Have a look at the multiple-choice items in the previous exercise. What did you do to increase your chances of getting a correct answer? Check (√) the methods that you used to find the answer.*
   1. ___ I used my general knowledge.
   2. ___ I eliminated the answers I knew were wrong.
   3. ___ I eliminated the answers that seemed illogical.
   4. ___ I looked for key words that appear both in the stem sentence and in the options.
   5. ___ Other (please specify).

Tips for Multiple-Choice Tests
- Read the directions carefully.
- From the directions, find out if the questions have one or more possible answers.
- Check how much time you have at your disposal.
- Preview all the questions.
- Start with the easiest ones.

- Then answer the more difficult questions.
- Review your answers at the end.

For more difficult questions
- Eliminate the options you know are incorrect
- Question the options that are completely unfamiliar
- Question the options that grammatically do not seem to fit with the stem sentence
- If two options are completely opposite, there are chances that one of them is correct
- If you have the option "All of the above" and two or three answers seem correct, then "All of the above" may well be the right answer.

9 *Do you usually apply any of the tips suggested when you have multiple-choice tests? If so, which ones? Which ones would you like to try? Discuss in small groups.*

Short-Answer Questions

True/false and *multiple-choice* questions require you to recognize correct and incorrect answers. *Short answer* tests, on the other hand, require you to formulate your own answer (usually factual information) as proof that you have general knowledge on the subject.

Preparing for Short-Answer Questions
- Make summary sheets/cards of the course materials (class notes and books)
- Pay special attention to key concepts and their meaning, dates and events, writers and information about their works (depending on the subject you prepare for this exam).
- Organize your material, then review.

Tips for Short-Answer Tests
- Read the question attentively.
- Pay attention to key words in the question that may restrict your answer.
- Give concise yet informative answers.

If, for example, in the *Literature* exam you have to answer the question "What is an epic?" what you need to do is give the definition of an epic and give some examples. If, on the other hand, you are asked to point out the differences between Part 1 and Part 3 in *Beowulf*, do not retell the poem and do not speak about its symbolism or its language; simply show how is Part 3 different from Part 1.

Essay Examinations

Essay examinations may be required either for a writing course or for a different course.

- In the former situation, the structure, organization, cohesion, coherence, support, clarity of expression are as important as content. You can have expectations regarding the type of essays you may be required to write (argumentative, process, classification, cause and effect, comparison and contrast, problem/solution, etc.), but you do not know what title the essay might have.
- When the essay is a form of examination for other courses, the content and clarity of expression are usually the most important elements. Many of the essay questions fall into these categories: argumentative, expository, comparison and contrast.

Tips for Essay Exams

? 10 *Below are some tips for successful essay examinations. Circle the number of those you feel are good advice. Compare your answers with two or three other students. What is the same? What is different?*

1. Decide how much time you have to answer each question.
2. Read the directions carefully, paying attention to key words and phrases, such as *compare*, *explain*, *summarize*, etc.
3. Generate ideas and make an outline before you write.
4. Write a strong, interesting first paragraph in which you express your main points.
5. Discuss each main point in a specific paragraph and support it with details, examples, quotations, facts and figures.
6. Begin each body paragraph with a key point from the introduction.
7. Use transitions to link your ideas and the points you make.
8. Write a conclusive paragraph in which you restate your main idea and summarize the main points you have made.
9. Allow time to review and complete your answers.
10. Allow time to correct grammar, spelling or punctuation mistakes.

Essay Question Directions

The second tip above advises you to read the directions very carefully. This is extremely important in the case of essay questions, because the essay instructions contain certain key words that tell you *how* to present the information.

?11 *Here are some terms that usually appear in essay exam directions. Match each term in column A with its definition in column B.*

A	B
1. ___compare	a. establish something with certainty based on experimental evidence or logical reasoning
2. ___contrast	b. clarify and interpret the subject you present, by trying to answer the questions *how* and *why*
3. ___define	c. give reasons based on evidence
4. ___describe	d. show differences
5. ___discuss	e. examine, analyze, present pros and cons
6. ___evaluate	f. characterize something or someone
7. ___explain	g. show similarities, resemblances
8. ___interpret	h. explain, exemplify, comment, give your judgment on the subject
9. ___justify	i. weigh and carefully appraise both advantages (strengths, contributions) and disadvantages (weaknesses, limitations)
10.___prove	j. give the main points or facts in a condensed manner
11.___summarize	k. give meaning of a certain word; identify concept, by showing the class it belongs to and what differentiates it from other members of the same class

國家圖書館出版品預行編目

Academic study skills: An introduction /
Nicoleta Mariana Iftimie, 張婉麗作. --
一版. -- 臺北市：秀威資訊科技, 民97
面; 公分-- (社會科學：AF0088)

ISBN 978-986-221-070-3(平裝)

520

 實踐大學數位出版合作系列
社會科學類　AF0088

Academic Study Skills: An Introduction

作　　者	Nicoleta Mariana Iftimie、張婉麗
統籌策劃	葉立誠
文字編輯	王雯珊
視覺設計	賴怡勳
執行編輯	賴敬暉
圖文排版	郭雅雯
數位轉譯	徐真玉　沈裕閔
圖書銷售	林怡君
法律顧問	毛國樑　律師
發 行 人	宋政坤
出版印製	秀威資訊科技股份有限公司
	台北市內湖區瑞光路583巷25號1樓
	電話：(02) 2657-9211
	傳真：(02) 2657-9106
	E-mail：service@showwe.com.tw
經 銷 商	紅螞蟻圖書有限公司
	台北市內湖區舊宗路二段121巷28、32號4樓
	電話：(02) 2795-3656
	傳真：(02) 2795-4100
	http://www.e-redant.com

2008 年 10 月
BOD一版
定價：260元

讀　者　回　函　卡

感謝您購買本書，為提升服務品質，煩請填寫以下問卷，收到您的寶貴意見後，我們會仔細收藏記錄並回贈紀念品，謝謝！

1.您購買的書名：＿＿＿＿＿＿＿＿＿＿＿＿＿＿＿＿＿＿＿

2.您從何得知本書的消息？

　□網路書店　□部落格　□資料庫搜尋　□書訊　□電子報　□書店

　□平面媒體　□ 朋友推薦　□網站推薦 □其他＿＿＿＿＿＿

3.您對本書的評價：(請填代號　1.非常滿意 2.滿意 3.尚可 4.再改進)

　封面設計＿＿＿　版面編排＿＿＿　內容＿＿＿　文/譯筆＿＿＿　價格＿＿＿

4.讀完書後您覺得：

　□很有收獲　□有收獲　□收獲不多　□沒收獲

5.您會推薦本書給朋友嗎？

　□會　□不會，為什麼？＿＿＿＿＿＿＿＿＿＿＿＿＿＿＿＿＿

6.其他寶貴的意見：＿＿＿＿＿＿＿＿＿＿＿＿＿＿＿＿＿＿＿

＿＿＿＿＿＿＿＿＿＿＿＿＿＿＿＿＿＿＿＿＿＿＿＿＿＿＿

＿＿＿＿＿＿＿＿＿＿＿＿＿＿＿＿＿＿＿＿＿＿＿＿＿＿＿

＿＿＿＿＿＿＿＿＿＿＿＿＿＿＿＿＿＿＿＿＿＿＿＿＿＿＿

讀者基本資料

姓名：＿＿＿＿＿＿＿＿＿＿　年齡：＿＿＿＿　性別：□女 □男

聯絡電話：＿＿＿＿＿＿＿＿　E-mail：＿＿＿＿＿＿＿＿＿＿

地址：＿＿＿＿＿＿＿＿＿＿＿＿＿＿＿＿＿＿＿＿＿＿＿＿＿

學歷：□高中(含)以下　　□高中　□專科學校　□大學

　　　□研究所(含)以上 □其他＿＿＿＿＿＿＿＿

職業：□製造業 □金融業 □資訊業 □軍警 □傳播業 □自由業

　　　□服務業 □公務員 □教職　□學生 □其他＿＿＿＿＿

To：114

台北市內湖區瑞光路 583 巷 25 號 1 樓

秀威資訊科技股份有限公司　　　收

寄件人姓名：

寄件人地址：□□□

(請沿線對摺寄回,謝謝!)

秀威與 BOD

BOD（Books On Demand）是數位出版的大趨勢，秀威資訊率先運用 POD 數位印刷設備來生產書籍，並提供作者全程數位出版服務，致使書籍產銷零庫存，知識傳承不絕版，目前已開闢以下書系：

一、BOD 學術著作—專業論述的閱讀延伸
二、BOD 個人著作—分享生命的心路歷程
三、BOD 旅遊著作—個人深度旅遊文學創作
四、BOD 大陸學者—大陸專業學者學術出版
五、POD 獨家經銷—數位產製的代發行書籍

BOD 秀威網路書店：www.showwe.com.tw
政府出版品網路書店：www.govbooks.com.tw

永不絕版的故事・自己寫・永不休止的音符・自己唱